THE ARTHUR OF HISTORY:

A REINTERPRETATION OF THE EVIDENCE

THE ARTHUR OF HISTORY

The Arthur of History: A Reinterpretation of the Evidence

Copyright © August Hunt September 1, 2015

Cover Photo: Members of the North British-based re-enactment group Comitatus, showing cavalry with a bearer of the draco standard. Courtesy Graham Sumner.

ABOUT THE AUTHOR

August Hunt has a lifelong passion for the Arthurian stories and has been studying them since his youth. He has lectured extensively on King Arthur at colleges and for re-enactment organizations. His articles on British Dark Age topics are also featured on various award-winning websites.

Drawing on his considerable knowledge of folklore, heroic legend and myth, as well as place-name studies, history and archaeology, August is providing new and challenging material which illuminates many of the previously shadowy areas of the Arthurian tradition.

August holds a degree in Celtic and Germanic Studies, and is a member of the International Arthurian Society. When he is not engaged in research and writing, he enjoys designing and building stone circles and other monuments that reproduce the celestial alignments of their ancient European counterparts.

His other Arthurian books include:

The Mysteries of Avalon: A Primer on Arthurian Druidism

THE ARTHUR OF HISTORY

THE ARTHUR OF HISTORY:

A REINTERPRETATION OF THE EVIDENCE

AUGUST HUNT

THE ARTHUR OF HISTORY

TO MY BROTHER, GALEN

For All of the Adventures

TABLE OF CONTENTS

ACKNOWLEDGMENTS	9
MAP OF BATTLE SITES	12
THE KING WHO ONCE WAS	13
BEFORE ARTHUR: AMBROSIUS, CUNEDDA AND VORTIGERN	24
ARTHUR'S ANCESTRY: RESTORING A GENEALOGY	46
THE BATTLES OF ARTHUR	84
ARTHUR'S OTHER BATTLES: MYTHOLOGICAL OR MISTAKEN	146
THE NORTHERN KINGDOMS	162
THE POWER CENTERS OF ARTHUR	189
THE GRAVE OF ARTHUR	209
THE KING WHO WILL BE AGAIN	214
APPENDIX I: CADBURYS AND BADBURYS	221
APPENDIX II: BIRDOSWALD RATHER THAN STANWIX AS ARTHUR'S CAPITAL	235
APPENDIX III: CAMLAN AND THE GRAVE OF OSFRAN'S SON	241
BIBLIOGRAPHY	249

THE ARTHUR OF HISTORY

"It is all true, or it ought to be; and more and better besides."

Sir Winston Churchill, on the legend of King Arthur

For friend and foe were shadows in the mist,
And friend slew friend not knowing whom he slew;
And some had visions out of golden youth,
And some beheld the faces of old ghosts Look in upon the battle; and in the mist
Was many a noble deed, many a base,
And chance and craft and strength in single fights
And ever and anon with host to host
Shocks, and the splintering spear; the hard mail hewn,
Shield-breakings, and the clash of brands, the crash
Of battleaxes on shattered helms, and shrieks
After the Christ, of those who falling down
Looked up for heaven, and only saw the mist;
And shouts of heathen and the traitor knights,
Oaths, insult, filth, and monstrous blasphemies,
Sweat, writhings, anguish, labouring of the lungs
In that close mist, and cryings for the light,
Moans of the dying, and voices of the dead.

'The Passing of Arthur' from Idylls of the King, Alfred Lord Tennyson

ACKNOWLEDGMENTS

I owe a great debt of gratitude to Dr. Richard Coates of the University of the West of England, Dr. Andrew Breeze of The University of Navarre and Dr. Isaac Graham of the National University of Ireland, Galway, for their acumen in treating of many word problems, tricky and obscure, and to Robert Vermaat, whose critical attention to many of my ideas often served to separate reasonable argument from mere fanciful construction. Finally, I would like to extend my heartfelt appreciation to photographer Ann Bowker, who literally climbed over hill and dale to get the photos that became such an integral part of this book, and to John Matthews, who not only supplied the excellent Foreword, but who offered much sage advice on revision of the manuscript. My heartfelt appreciation also goes out to the following correspondents, whose kindness, patience and dedication helped me put the pieces of the Arthurian puzzle together: Elizabeth O'Brien, UCD Mícheál Ó Cléirigh Institute; Andrew Hawke, National Dictionary of Wales; Peter Wihl, Carmarthenshire place-name expert; Dafydd Hawkins, Powys place-name expert; Kevin Coyle, University of Ottawa; Paul Cavill, The English Place-Name Society; Chris Chandler of English Heritage; Andrew Deathe, Salisbury Museum; Hywel Wyn Owen, University of Wales, Bangor; Richard Coates, University of the West of England; Padraig O Riain, University College, Cork; Sigmund Eisner, University of Arizona, Emeritus; Gareth Bevans, National Library of Wales; Hoyt Greeson, Department of

English, Laurentian University; Paul Acker, Saint Louis University; Gregory S. Uchrin, Catholic University of America; Jean-Yves le Moing; Christian Rogel, Director of the Bibliotheque du Finistere, Quimper; Helen McBurnie, Cramlington Parish Secretary; Neil Moffat, Reference and Local Studies Department, Dumfries and Galloway Libraries, Information and Archives, Dumfries and Galloway Council; Peter Drummond, Scottish Place-Name Society; Mark Douglas, Principal Officer for Heritage and Design, Planning and Economic Development, Scottish Borders Council; Nicola Hunt, Projects Officer of the Borders Forest Trust; Helen Darling, Part-Time Local Studies Librarian, Library Headquarters, St. Mary's Hill, Selkirk; Jennifer Parkson, Map Library, Assistant for the National Library of Scotland; Henry Gough Cooper, Scottish Place-Name Society; Neil Bettridge, Archivist, Derbyshire County Council's Record Office; John Reid, Scottish Place-Name Society; Beatrix Faerber, CELT Project Manager; Ceridwen Lloyd-Morgan, Assistant Archivist, Department of Manuscripts and Records, The National Library of Wales; Brynley F. Roberts, Centre for Advanced Welsh and Celtic Studies, University of Wales; Patrick Sims-Williams, University of Wales; Bruce Jackson, Lancashire County Archivist; Humphrey Welfare, Planning and Development Director, North, English Heritage; Richard Annis, Durham University's Project manager of Archaeological Services; Tim Padley, Keeper of Archaeology, Tullie House Museum and Art Gallery, Carlisle; Georgina Plowright, Curator English Heritage Hadrian's Wall Museums; Stephen White, Carlisle Library; Robert

Collins, Newcastle Upon Tyne Museum of Antiquities; Kevan W. White of roman-britain.org; Gill Stroud, Sites and Monument Records Officer, Derbyshire County Council; Ken Smith, Cultural Heritage Manager for the Peak District National Park Authority; John Moreland, Reader at the University of Sheffield, Department of Archaeology' Sue Palmer, Assistant Museums Manager of the Buxton Museum and Art Gallery, Oliver J. Padel, Cambridge University.

THE ARTHUR OF HISTORY

THE BATTLE SITES OF ARTHUR, ALONG WITH POWER CENTER AND TRADITIONAL BURIAL PLACE

INTRODUCTION

THE KING WHO ONCE WAS

What little we know of an 'historical' Arthur is contained in two early medieval works: the Historia Brittonum* or History of the Britons, ascribed to the Welsh monk Nennius, and the anonymous Annales Cambriae or Welsh Annals. These two sources supply us with the names of thirteen Arthurian battle sites. Twelve of these battles were supposedly fought against the invading Saxons, while one may have involved a conflict with another British chieftain named Medraut, the Mordred of later Arthurian romance.

The first twelve of these battles are all found in the HB immediately after mention of Aesc son of Hengist's rise to the kingship in Kent, an event dated to 488 CE in the Anglo-Saxon Chronicle, and just prior to a section dealing with the Saxon kingdom of Bernicia and its king, Ida. Bernicia, coupled with Deira, comprised what became known as Northumbria, i.e. that portion of Britain that extends from the Humber River in the south to the Firth of Forth in the north. Ida began to rule, according to the ASC, circa 547 CE.

Camlann, the thirteenth battle, is found only in the AC, where it is dated to 537 CE. Thus the thirteen battles of Arthur are chronologically fixed within the period of 488 to 547 CE or from the latter part of the 5th century to the middle of the 6th. While several alternate chronologies have been proposed for the ASC and certain entries of the AC, for the sake of clarity the traditional dates will be allowed to stand.

The list of Arthurian battle sites, in the order that they occur in the HB and the AC, are as follows:

1) ostium fluminis quod dicitur Glein, mouth of the river Glein
2), 3), 4) & 5) flumen quod dicitur Dubglas, et est in regione Linnuis, river Dubglas in the Linnuis region 6) flumen quod vocatur Bassas, river Bassas
7) silva Celidonis, id est Cat Coit Celidon, Celidon Wood, Battle of Celidon Wood
8) castello Guinnion, castle of Guinnion
9) urbe Legionis, City of the Legion
10) litore fluminis quod vocatur Tribruit, river-shore Tribruit
11) monte qui dicitur Agned, mount Agned or monte qui nominator Breguoin, mount Breguoin
12) Badonis (AC), monte Badonis (HB), mount Badon (cf. Badonici montis of Gildas, who first mentioned Badon in his 6th century work, De Excidio Brittonum, The Ruin of Britain)
13) Camlann (AC), Camlan

In the HB, Arthur is called a dux bellorum or 'leader of battles', and is said to have fought alongside British kings against the pagan barbarians. It is from this bare listing of battle sites that the great body of Arthurian literature – the so-called 'Matter of Britain' – has grown. The consensus view among Arthurian scholars today is that the subsequent poems, stories, pseudo-histories and romances focusing on Arthur and his court are so heavily fictionalized, so overlaid with mythic, legendary and folkloristic elements, as to be worthless for the study of Arthur as a true Dark Age personage.

There are even those who dispense with the HB and AC Arthurian accounts as well, claiming that there is no way for us to substantiate the genuineness of either.

Some scholars go even further in refusing to accept as historically viable in entirety the HB or AC themselves. Indeed, to many the HB is no more than a hodge-podge of historical traditions which in all likelihood has little bearing on the actual events that transpired in Dark Age Britain.

A complication concerns the inability to clearly identify the place-names supplied in the battle list. The tendency has existed for some time to 'make the places fit the theory', rather than the opposite. Thus Arthur has been situated just about everywhere in Britain. Artificial geographical patterns have been sought for the battles in order to pinpoint Arthur's power centre and shed dubious light on his origins. Sound philological principles have all too often gone by the wayside when treating of Arthurian place-names. It is precisely the inability to satisfactorily pin down Arthur's battles that has led some scholars to give up the quest and join with those who insist on his non-historicity. For without firm battle site identifications, nothing of the historical Arthur can be known.

THE ARTHUR OF HISTORY

* Abbreviations: HB (Historia Brittonum), AC (Annales Cambriae) and ASC (Anglo-Saxon Chronicle) in future references.

To counter the argument that refuses to acknowledge the validity of the battle list, the two Arthurian entries in the AC have frequently been cited. These entries are typical, dry, bare-boned annalistic accounts of battles. Arthur, Medraut and the battle sites of Mt. Badon and Camlan are mentioned in the context of many other proper and place-names, all of which are demonstrably historical in nature. According to this line of reasoning, we need not doubt the veracity of the two entries.

516 an. Bellum Badonis, in quo Arthur portavit crucem Domini nostri Jesu Christi tribus diebus et tribus noctibus in humeros suos et Brittones victores fuerunt.

"The Battle of Badon, in which Arthur carried the cross of our Lord Jesus Christ for three days and three nights on his shoulders and the Britons were the victors."

537 an. Gueith Camlann in quo Arthur et Medraut corruerunt, et mortalitas in Brittannia et Hibernia fuit.

"The Battle of Camlan, in which Arthur and Medraut fell, and there was plague in Britain and Ireland."

Mt. Badon and Camlan are both, however, subject to the same kind of geographical shuffling as the other battle sites. Cases have been made for northern and southern Badons and Camlans. Few have been particularly convincing. Also, what may be legendary accretions similar to those present in the HB's description of Arthur's battle at Castellum Guinnion are to be found in the AC entry on Badon.

Octavum fuit bellum in castello Guinnion, in quo Arthur portavit imaginem sanctae Mariae perpetuae virginis super humeros suos, et pagani versi sunt in fugam in illo die, et caedes magna fuit super illos per virtutem Domini nostri Jesu Christi et per virtutem sanctae Mariae virginis benetreis ejus.

"The eighth battle was in Castle Guinnion, and in it Arthur carried the image of the holy Mary, the everlasting Virgin, on his [shield], and the heathen were put to flight on that day, and there was a great slaughter of them, through the power of our Lord Jesus Christ and the power of the holy Virgin Mary, his mother."

Such embellishments have convinced many that the Badon entry in the AC should be disqualified as a record of a true Arthurian battle. In this case, it can be plausibly argued that the AC Badon entry has been contaminated by the HB's account of Arthur's battle at Castle Guinnion. This is not to say that Badon itself is denied status as an historical event; only that the placement of Arthur at Gildas's Badon should be interpreted as an instance of hero-making and nothing more.

Gildas himself neglected to include in his work the name of the British commander at Badon:

26. ... usque ad annum obsessionis Badonici montis, novissimaeque ferme de furciferis non minimae stragis...

"This lasted right up till the year of the siege of Mount Badon, pretty well the last defeat of the villains, and certainly not the least."

Admittedly, in recent years there has been a sort of cautious reaction to the views set forth by proponents of a non-historical Arthur. While respecting the limitations imposed by the nature of the earliest Arthurian sources, limitations that the critical analysis of texts has largely defined, a handful of scholars have made significant headway in dealing with what they believe to be a fundamental over-statement of the problem of Arthur's historicity. These scholars do not object to the actual process of critical analysis, but to some of the conclusions that have been drawn from the results of such analysis. The said conclusions, when treated of logically, can be revealed as arbitrarily formed and thus are reflections of expert opinion or even prejudice or bias, and not objective fact.

The 'Arthur Problem', put in the simplest terms, is this: is there sufficient reason for seeing the Arthur of the HB and AC as a plausible historical entity? Those who choose to see Arthur as a non-historical personage may strenuously object to this question. They would doubtless prefer that the problem be stated differently, e.g. is there sufficient evidence for seeing the Arthur of the sources as a historical entity?

Unfortunately, demanding evidence of the kind that would satisfy the proponents of the non-historical view automatically removes Arthur from the realm of historical study. Happening upon complimentary textual evidence from a source or sources deemed authentic and dependable seems a remote possibility. Archaeology, despite the ever-increasing light it sheds on Britain's Dark Age past, has so far failed to yield anything substantive on Arthur. By refusing to allow for the possibility that Arthur may conceivably be historical, scholars engage in a sort of self-fulfilling prophecy, the fulfillment of which can only be that Arthur will continue to be found ineligible for historical status. Along with maintaining such perpetual ineligibility is a steadfast refusal on the part of scholars to allow interested parties to engage in research that might be deemed related even tangentially to Arthur as a possible historical phenomenon.

It may ultimately prove true that the only value in further analysis of Arthur's battle sites might be an elucidation of the 9th century's perspective on and attitude towards a reputed 5th-6th century British war-leader. Granted, there is some indication that the battle list as found in the HB is not an artificial construction undertaken by the monk Nennius, but instead preserves the content, rather than strictly the form, of a much earlier heroic poem originally composed in Arthur's honor. If this widely held view is correct, then the battle list may reflect something other than a late traditional portrait of Arthur. It may be much more of a contemporary record of campaigns than the 9th century source in which it is embedded might otherwise suggest.

Still, if findings that arise from additional probing into the probable locations of Arthurian battle sites accomplish nothing other than to bring more into focus how the 9th century Britons interpreted their own remote past, then we will still have greatly advanced our knowledge of the period.

The burden of proof is just as much on the shoulders of those who dismiss Arthur as non-historical as it is on those who conditionally accept him as historical. Such an acknowledgment forces us to accept the possibility that Arthur existed without having to entertain the probability. If it can be demonstrated, based upon our knowledge of his battles, that an Arthur in the time period under consideration is a plausible phenomenon, then we can open a doorway into new areas of intellectual endeavor whose express purpose is to provide the impetus for the eventual discovery of evidence needed to historicize this British war-leader.

If there were to be an implied philosophy underlying this book, it would be that scholars of Arthuriana or Dark Age Britain ought not to view with disdain objective exploration of the potential historicity of Arthur. For as it may well turn out, the sources we do possess for the military career of this Dark Age figure may prove to have validity after all. While the means of providing such validity are currently not available to us, to state as fact that Arthur is not a historical entity or that we are not justified in seeing him as being even plausibly historical, is to risk making one of the biggest blunders imaginable in the annals of academic investigation.

It is the business of Arthurian and Dark Age scholars to consider possibilities. By possibilities is not meant, of course, wild theories that have no hope of ever being substantiated. Instead, possibilities in this context can best be defined as plausible historic scenarios that, while they may not be testable at the moment, may prove to be so in the future. Such scenarios must, needless to say, fit into the general, though wonderfully complex and interdependent tapestry created for us by universally accepted disciplines of study.

As more and more data comes in from these disciplines, and the resulting picture of the past is altered or refined accordingly, those scenarios that fail to conform in a manner deemed appropriate can be dispensed with. Eventually, with the aid of increasingly sophisticated scientific tools, our knowledge of Dark Age British history will be much greater than it is now. Most plausible scenarios will have been discarded. An historical Arthur might well be one of these casualties. Only a few scenarios – perhaps, if we are extraordinarily fortunate, just one – will remain solvent.

But until then, summarily deleting Arthur from the pages of our history books is not an ethical or reasonable solution to the 'Arthur Problem'. It would be wiser and less shortsighted to include him, albeit with the necessary caveats. Any further evidence that supported Arthur's historicity could thus be uncovered earlier, rather than later.

The present book, therefore, operates under the premise that precisely because Arthur may be historical, it would be intellectually prudent to apply more effort to the study of the only textual evidence we do have regarding this Dark Age British war-leader, i.e. the battles listed in the HB and AC. On the other hand, to ignore the battles themselves as possible historical events would be to intentionally turn a blind eye to evidence that has not yet been thoroughly evaluated. Potentially, a comprehensive examination of the battle sites, if undertaken with no agenda, nationalistic or otherwise, might harvest some new information on Arthur. And any new information, whether it ends up contributing arguments for or against a historical personage, is the proper goal of true scholarship.

The method employed by the author will be to utilize sound philological and geographical principles in the context of the Arthurian battles in order to arrive at several new site identifications. Included in this analysis, by necessity, will be a brief consideration of those past and present identifications deemed to be of a more respectable nature. But first will come some speculation regarding the period just before Arthur, with special emphasis on the figures of Ambrosius, Cunedda and Vortigern. Arthur's origins will then be explored, utilizing the earliest versions of ancient Welsh genealogies, as well as the etymology of the name Arthur and its historical attestations in both Roman and Dark Age Britain. The remainder of the book will explore the Dark Age British kingdoms in the North and the power centres and grave of Arthur. These various investigations will produce a theoretical reconstruction of the life and death of 'King Arthur'.

The reader should understand that many proper and place-name authorities have been consulted in the preparation of this book, either via personal correspondence or through their published works or both, and I have listed these generous and often patient contributors on my Acknowledgments page and in the Bibliography. Any conclusions I have drawn by relying on scholarly elucidation are solely my own and do not in any way reflect the opinions of the scholars themselves.

CHAPTER 1

BEFORE ARTHUR: AMBROSIUS, CUNEDDA AND VORTIGERN

Ambrosius

Aurelius Ambrosius, said to be a Roman, is the most famous figure in Dark Age British history prior to Arthur. Why? Because he is credited with having united the Britons in a successful defense of the country against the Saxons, who from Vortigern's time had, according to the traditional account, pillaged and conquered at will.

Ambrosius is important also because it has been fashionable to identify him with Arthur. As we shall see, such an identification is patently impossible.

To begin, Ambrosius was not a contemporary of Arthur. He was not, in fact, even a contemporary of Vortigern, who preceded Arthur by a century. And this is true despite the HB account, which brings Vortigern and Ambrosius (as the Welsh Emrys) together for a fabulous story that takes place at Dinas Emrys in northwestern Wales (see below).

There are major problems with accepting Ambrosius as a contemporary of Vortigern. First, he cannot have been a Roman and been in Britain during or after Vortigern's rule. The withdrawal of the Romans is firmly dated at c. 409 CE. Vortigern's ruling dates, depending on the sources consulted, are anywhere from twenty to forty years after the Roman withdrawal. If he were a Roman during or after Vortigern, then he came from the Continent and was not a native Briton. The argument could be made that 'Romanized' Britons continued to preserve the Roman way of life in southern England for a half century after the withdrawal of the troops. In this sense, a chieftain like Ambrosius might still consider himself to be 'Roman'.

However, the HB tells us that Ambrosius fought a battle against a certain Vitalinus at a Guoloph or Wallop, thought to be the Hampshire Wallop. This Vitalinus is listed in the HB as the grandfather of Vortigern. This means that Ambrosius has wrongly been placed in the time of Vortigern. He actually belongs to the time of Vitalinus, who was probably of the 4th century.

The father of the famous 4th century St. Ambrose bore the name Aurelius Ambrosius. This man was, furthermore, the prefect or governor of Gaul (Gallia). Britain, Spain and Gaul were in the Gallic prefecture. So, we have here a historical figure named Aurelius Ambrosius who not only was a true 'Roman', but who could have had something to do with military operations carried out in Britain in the 4th century.

There is good reason to believe that St. Ambrose himself bore the name Aurelius. Jones' Prosopography of the Later Roman Empire gives no second name for the bishop of Milan and neither does Paulinus of Milan's Vita. Ambrose may have belonged to the gens Aurelia, as we know that he was related to Symmachus [Quintus Aurelius Symmachus]; an inscription refers to him as Aurelius Ambrosius. It is true that there is a debate over the Ambrose referred to in the inscription. Those who think it is Ambrose junior [St. Ambrose] point out that a dedication to St. Nazarius is involved. The point may be moot: if Ambrose senior belonged to the gens Aurelia, so did the son, and vice versa.

One other factor strongly indicates that there is no good historical reason for accepting a 5th century Aurelius Ambrosius in Britain. Vortigern's only interaction with Ambrosius, or Emrys Guletic ('Prince Ambrosius') as he is called in Welsh tradition, is in the Dinas Emrys folktale already alluded to above.

Other than Dinas Emrys, there appears to be no site in Britain which can be shown to contain the personal name Ambrosius. Still, this hero may even have been placed at Guoloph/Wallop because of the proximity of this stream to Amesbury. As Geoffrey of Monmouth did much later, Ambrosius's name was fancifully associated with Amesbury.

The town name does not, in fact, seem to contain the personal name Ambrosius. Its etymology is instead as follows:

Ambresbyrig, from a c.880 CE charter, then various spellings to Amblesberie in Domesday. Almost certainly a personal name Ambre or Aembre cognate with the Old German Ambri, hence Ambre's burgh, cf. Ombersley. All the early forms for Amesbury have the medial -b-, but no form has any extension that would justify derivation from Ambrosius.

Ambrosius as a Latin adjective means "the Divine or Immortal One". As such, it was at some point taken to be a title for the Welsh god Lleu. Welsh tradition made Lleu the ancient ruler of Gwynedd, and this is the rank granted to Emrys or Ambrosius in the HB. Hence Dinas Emrys in northwestern Wales, the '[Hill-] fort of the Divine or Immortal One', is actually the Fort of Lleu.

The Welsh also appear to have identified the youthful god Mabon with Lleu. That this is so is demonstrated by the placement of the two gods in death at the same place. According to the Mabinogion tale Math Son of Mathonwy, Lleu is found as the death-eagle in the oak tree at Nantlle (Nant Lleu) in Snowdonia not far from Dinas Emrys. And one of the Stanzas of the Graves reads:

"The grave on Nantlle's height, No one knows its attributes – Mabon son of Modron the Swift."

In Chapter 6, we will discuss Emrys's Campus Elleti, supposedly a site in southern Wales, in the context of Camelot.

Geoffrey of Monmouth proceeded to further confuse the story of Ambrosius, a Roman governor of Gaul mistakenly identified with a Welsh god, by identifying both with the Northern Myrddin or Merlin. Hence we find Merlin or 'Merlin Ambrosius' in the Dinas Emrys story of Emrys/Lleu/Mabon.

In addition, Merlin is placed at the springs of Galabes, Geoffrey's attempt at the Guoloph of the hero Ambrosius.

In conclusion, we can only say that there is no good reason for supposing that Vortigern and Ambrosius were contemporaries. Instead, the Ambrosius mentioned by Gildas as having military success in Britian must have been the 4th century Gallic governor of that name. This being the case, Ambrosius could not possibly have been the victor at the battle of Mount Badon, which is dated 516 CE. And, by extension, Ambrosius was not Arthur.

Cunedda

The great Cunedda, called Cunedag (supposedly from *Cunodagos, 'Good Hound') in the Historia Brittonum, is said to have come down (or been brought down) from Manau Gododdin, a region around the head of the Firth of Forth, to Gwynedd. This chieftain and his sons then, according to the account found in the HB, proceeded to repulse Irish invaders. Unfortunately, this tradition is largely mistaken. To prove that this is so, we need to begin by looking at the famous Wroxeter Stone, found at the Viroconium Roman fort in what had been the ancient kingdom of the Cornovii, but which was the kingdom of Powys in the Dark Ages.

The Wroxeter Stone is a memorial to a chieftain named Cunorix son of Maquicoline. This stone has been dated c. 460-75 CE. Maquicoline is a composite name meaning Son [Maqui-] of Coline. The resemblance here of Cunorix and Coline to the ASC's Cynric and his son Ceawlin is obvious. Some scholars would doubtless say this is coincidence, and that the discrepancy in dates for Cynric and Ceawlin and Cunorix and (Maqui)coline are too great to allow for an identification. I would say that an argument based on the very uncertain ASC dates is hazardous at best and that if there is indeed a relationship between the pairs Ceawlin-Cynric and Coline-Cunorix, then the date of the memorial stone must be favored over that of the document.

There is also the problem of Cynric being the father of Ceawlin in the Anglo-Saxon tradition, while on the Wroxeter Stone it is (Maqui)coline who is the father of Cunorix. But such a confusion could easily have occurred simply by reading part of a genealogy list backwards.

While Ceawlin's father Cynric, the son of Cerdic of Wessex in most pedigrees, is capable of being derived quite well from Anglo-Saxon, the name could also be construed as an Anglicized form of the attested Celtic name Cunorix, Hound-king, the latter Welsh Cynyr.

Cerdic (= Ceredig) is not the only Celtic name in the early Wessex pedigree. Scholars have suggested that Ceawlin could be Brittonic.

Cunorix son of Maquicoline, based on an analysis of his name and the lettering employed on the inscription itself, is believed to have been Irish. It should not surprise us, then, to find Cunedda of Manau Gododdin, the reputed founder of Gwynedd, was himself actually Irish. There was an early St. Cuindid (d. c. 497 CE) son of Cathbad, who founded a monastery at Lusk, ancient Lusca. In the year entry 498 CE of the Ulster Annals, his name is spelled in the genitive as Chuinnedha. In Tigernach 496 CE, the name is Cuindedha.

The Irish sources also have the following additional information concerning St. Cuindid:

Mac Cuilind - Cunnid proprium nomen - m. Cathmoga m. Cathbath m Cattain m Fergossa m. Findchada m Feic m. Findchain m Imchada Ulaig m. Condlai m Taide m. Cein m Ailella Olum.

U496.2 Quies M. Cuilinn episcopi Luscan. (Repose of Mac Cuilinn, bishop of Lusca).

D.viii. idus Septembris. 993] Luscai la Macc Cuilinn

994] caín decheng ad-rannai, 995] féil Scéthe sund linni, 996] Coluimb Roiss gil Glandai.

trans: 'With Macc cuilinn of Luscae thou apportionest (?) a fair couple: the feast of Sciath here we have, (and that) of Columb of bright Ross Glandae'

The (later-dated) notes to this entry read: 'Lusk, i.e. in Fingall, i.e. a house that was built of weeds (lusrad) was there formerly, and hence the place is named Lusca ....Macc cuilinn, i.e. Luachan mac cuilinn, ut alii putant. Cuinnid was his name at first, Cathmog his father's name'.

Significantly, Lusk or Lusca is a very short distance from the huge promontory fort at Drumanagh, the Bruidhne Forgall Manach of the ancient Irish tales. Drumanagh is the hill of the Manapii and, as such, represents the Manapia in Manapii territory found on the map of Ptolemy. Manapii or Manapia could easily have been mistaken or substituted for for the Manau in Gododdin.

Aeternus, Cunedda's father, is none other than Aithirne of Dun and Ben Etair just south of Lusca. Paternus Pesrudd ('Red-Cloak'), Cunedda's grandfather, is probably not derived from Mac Badairn of Es Ruad ('Red Waterfall'), since Es Ruad is in northwest Ireland (Ballyshannon in Co. Donegal). I think Paternus, from the L. word for 'father', is Da Derga, the Red God; Da, god, being interpreted as W. tad (cf. L. tata, 'father'). The Da Derga's hostel was just a little south of the Liffey. Cunedda's great-great-grandfather is said to be one Tegid (Tacitus), while his great-great-great grandfather is called Cein. These two chieftains are clearly Taig/Tadhg and his father Cian. Cian was the founder of the Irish tribe the Ciannachta, who ruled Mag Breg, a region situated between the Liffey and either Duleek or Drumiskin (depending on the authority consulted). The Lusca and Manapia of Chuinnedha are located in Mag Breg.

According to the genealogy edited in Corpus Genealogiarum Sanctorum Hiberniae, the name of Mac Cuilind's father was Cathmug. He belonged to the descendants of Tadc mac Cian, otherwise called the Cianachta. There was a concentration of the saints of this family in the Dublin/Louth/Meath area, corresponding roughly to the teritory of the Cianachta Breg.

It is surely not a coincidence that according to the Irish Annals Chuinnedha's other name was Mac Cuilinn. Obviously, Mac Cuilinn and the Maqui-Coline of the Wroxeter Stone are the same name and hence the same person. Gwynedd was thus founded by Chuinnedha alias Mac Cuilinn of the Manapii in Ireland, not by a chieftain of Manau Gododdin in Britain.

The Irish origin of Cunedda should not be a surprise to us, as there is the well-documented case of the Welsh genealogy of the royal house of Dyfed, which was altered to hide the fact that Dyfed was founded by the Irish Deisi. We know this because we have the corresponding Irish genealogy from a saga which tells of the expulsion of the Deisi from Ireland and their settlement in Dyfed. As is true of Cunedda's pedigree, in the Welsh Dyfed pedigree we find Roman names substituted for Irish names. There were other Irish-founded kingdoms in Wales as well, e.g. Brycheiniog.

What exactly the relationship was that existed between Cunedda and the British kingdom of Powys on the one hand, and Cunedda/Ceawlin of the Gewissei and the Saxons of southern England on the other, is something that can only be surmised once we plug Vortigern into the equation. While it is true that Bede called Ceawlin a Bretwalda, i.e. a preeminent ruler of Britain, we are not justified in equating him with Vortigern.

Vortigern

The name Vortigern or Gwrtheyrn, as found in the HB of Nennius, was once held to be a ruling title. It was thought to be represented by Gildas' Latin pun 'superbus tyrannus' or 'Proud Tyrant'. However, we now know that Vortigern was a proper name and not a title. It is found recorded not only in several localities in Wales, but in Ireland as well.

Aside from the British Vortigern, whose name means 'Over-lord', we have records for the following Dark Age Irish Vortigerns or 'Fortcherns':

1) Fortchern, the smith of St. Patrick (Annals of the Four Masters Year Entry 448); as this Fortchern is paired with another smith, Laebhan, i.e. St. Lomman (?), this Fortchern may be:

2) Foirtchern son of Fedelmid, who was for a short time bishop of St. Lomman's Trim. Fortchern of Trim, who was of mixed Irish and British blood, is said to have later retired to Killoughterane/Cill Fortchern in the parish of

Muinebeag, Co. Carlow. However, we are told in the ancient Irish sources that Fortchern the smith is the same as Foirtchern of Rath Seimhne (see below). It may not be a coincidence that there is a Gobbin's Cliff, the Cliffs of the divine smith Goban Saor, in Seimhne/Island Magee.
3) Vortigern of Ballyhank, East Muskerry, Co. Cork (inscribed stone).
4) Vortigern of Knockboy in Decies Without Drum, Co. Waterford (inscribed stone dated c. 700-900 CE).
5) Foirtchern of Monte Cainle (probably the Hill of Conlig/Coinleac in north Co. Down), a contemporary of St. Columba.
6) Foirtchern of Rath Seimhne (Island Magee, south Co. Antrim).
7) Fortchern, brother of Cathchern (a name cognate with British Cattigern, a supposed son of Vortigern in the HB narrative), son of Tigernach of the Meic Carthind of the Lough Foyle region.
8) Fortcheirn son of Mael Rubae of the Ui Dicholla of the Dessi
9) Fortchern son of Iarlaith of the Ui Brigte of the Dessi
10) Fortchern son of Tigernach of the Ui Brigte of the Dessi
11) Clan Foirtchern in the Breadach genealogy on Inishowen, near the Lough Foyle Meic Carthind

These examples, some 'in stone', should be sufficient to dispell the notion that Vortigern is merely a title. Instead, Vortigern is a genuine Brythonic personal name.

In Wales, Radnorshire or Maesyfed (the 'field of Hyfaidd') was once known as Gwrtheyrnion, i.e. the kingdom of Gwrtheyrn. Gwrtheyrnion, roughly between the Wye and Ithon rivers, was a relatively small kingdom in southwestern Powys. Other places in Wales where Vortigern's name is preserved are Nant Gwrtheyrn in Lleyn, close to Gwyniasa (and surrounding Gwynus place-names), and a Craig Gwrtheyrn on the Teifi.

These three places are mentioned in Nennius's narrative, but only Gwrtheyrnion carries weight. The Lleyn and Teifi sites may represent the presence in these places of other Vortigerns, but in all likelihood it is merely the proximity to them of St. Garmon place-names that accounts for the 'Over-lord's' association with them. In Nennius's story of Vortigern, the poor chieftain is literally hounded all over Wales by the saint. Thus wherever there was a known St. Garmon site, Vortigern was placed there. In my opinion, Vortigern was probably not in Lleyn, nor was he on the Teifi (despite the presence at nearby Nevern of a Vitalinus Stone; see below). He belonged instead to Gwrtheyrnion, which was merely one of several Welsh Dark Age sub-kingdoms.

Vortigern of Wales, who is said to have been the son of Guitaul (= Roman Vitalis) son of Guitolin (= Roman Vitalinus, a name found on a stone at Nevern dated by Charles Thomas between 466 and 533 CE – too late for Vortigern's grandfather) son of Gloiu (Gloyw, the eponym of Welsh Caerloyw, modern Gloucester), is actually the British-Irish Fortchern son of Fedelmid son of Laeghaire. This Fortchern son of Fedelmid was of the right time to be the Vortigern of Nennius. Both Guitaul and Guitolin are substituted for the name Fedel-mid.

It was Robert Vermaat who first called my attention to the details surrounding this particular Fortchern. To quote extensively from his Vortigern Studies website article,

'Scotnoe & Foirtgirn, the Irish Branch':

"Foirtchern was the son of Fedelmid, son of Loguire, who was High King of Ireland throughout the period of the mission of St. Patrick (whose dates may be 428-462). Foirtchern's mother was a daughter of the King of the Britons. The story goes that when St. Patrick's nephew Lomman visited Trim (in Ireland), the boy Foirtchernn took him home to Fedelmid and his mother, who both spoke British and were delighted to see a visitor from his mother's country. They made Lomman stay, who then subsequently converted the whole family. The mother might have been a Christian in the first place, for she 'welcomed' the saint. Maybe the fact that Lomman was a Christian made him more welcome than his being from Britain. Fedelmid may have embraced Christianity because the saint had just come from Tara Hill, where St. Patrick had defeated the druids of Fedelmid's father the High King Loguire.

Foirtchern's date may be confirmed by the Annala Rioghachta Eirann:

Annals of the Four Masters, M432.0 – 4

The Age of Christ, 432. The fourth year of Laeghaire. Patrick came to Ireland this year, and proceeded to baptize and bless the Irish, men, women, sons, and daughters, except a few who did not consent to receive faith or baptism from him, as his Life relates. Ath Truim was founded by Patrick, it having been granted by Fedhlim, son of Laeghaire, son of Niall, to God and to him, Loman, and Fortchern.

These annals, though dating to 1616 in their youngest version, date back at least to 1172.

In any case, Fedelmid enthrusted Foirtchirnn to Lomman and founded the church of Trim, making St Patrick, Lomman and Foirtchirnn his heirs. But Foirtchernn was obdurate and did not want to accept his heritage, after which Lomman had to threaten him with taking away the blessing of the church, which is tantamount to incurring its curse. After Lomman's death, though, Foirtchirnn gave away his church within three days. This may be apocryphal, for Foirtchirnn was listed afterwards as the first episcopus (abbot) after Fedelmid and Lomman. He might have given it up later though, for he is also listed as a plebilis, a lay successor."

Now, the question on my mind, after reading this account, was "Who succeeded Lomman at Trim?" The answer is in the Patrician Texts in the Book of Armagh:

He [Foirtchernn] held the abbacy for three days after his master's death until he came to Ath

Truim, and then immediately handed his church over to the foreigner Cathlaid [Cathlaido perigrino].

I immediately recognized this 'Cathlaid the Foreigner' as a doublet for Catel Durnluc, the traditional founder of Powys, the kingdom that succeeded that of the Roman-period Cornovii.

Fortchern son of Fedelmid's mixed ancestry allows for the possibility that he possessed or inherited lands on both sides of the Irish Sea. We know that there were several Irish-founded kingdoms in Wales at the time: the Deissi established a ruling dynasty in Dyfed, Brycheiniog was of Irish foundation, and Cunedda of Manau Gododdin, founder of Gwynedd, was actually Chuinnedha/MacCuilind of Drum Managh in Ireland. Cunedda and his sons are said to have chased the Irish Ui Liathain out of Anglesey, Dyfed, Gower and Kidwelly, the Laigin were at Dinllaen and in the Lleyn Peninsula, and there is the possibility that Dinevor in Ystrad Tywi was named for an Efwr Llwydon, i.e. of the Irish Laithain. The Irish mercenary Cunorix son of Maquicoline/Cunedda was buried in the heart of Powys at Viroconium. There is no difficulty, then, in accepting a Gwrtheyrnion as a sub-kingdom named after Fortchern son of Fedelmid.

The only objection to a Gwrtherynion ruled by a chieftain of mixed British-Irish ancestry would be that such a king, with such a small sub-kingdom, could not possibly be the 'superbus tyrannus' of Gildas. But I offer this argument to account for how such a confusion could have taken place: any chieftain possessing a name such Vor-tigern, 'the over-/super-/great- lord' could easily have been misinterpreted as an over-king similar to the ardrigh or 'high-king' of Ireland. If I am right and Fortchern son of Fedelmid son of Laeghaire the high king is the British Vortigern of Gwrtheyrnion, then this kind of royal descent from an ardrigh could also have contributed to Gildas's misinterpretation of Vortigern's status in Britain.

In summary, then, what may have happened is this: a chieftain named Vortigern (or Fortchern), who was of mixed Irish-British ancestry, and whose grandfather was the ardrigh of Ireland, had established a small sub-kingdom in south-western Powys in the 5th century. Gildas, attracted to the name because it seemed to denote a sort of British high king, laid the blame for the Saxon 'invitation' (i.e. the use of Germanic barbarian federates) in this presumed high king's lap. Further vilification continued after this identification of Vortigern as the offending monarch was made, until by the 9th century we have a fully developed story of Vortigern in the HB of Nennius.

Alternately, given that the Eliseg Pillar in what was the kingdom of Powys traces the descent of the Powys dynasty from Vortigern, and Catel Durnluc is in the various genealogies confused with Vortigern or made his near-descendent, it is possible that Fortchern son of Fedelmid, at least partly through his wife's British blood, had managed to lay claim to the throne of Powys itself. His sub-kingdom of Gwrtheyrnion was, after all, part of Powys.

A final possibility, and one which calls into some doubt the notion that Vortigern was related to the Irish high king, is the proximity of Gwrtheyrnion to Brycheiniog. The latter, as Charles Thomas has shown in his 'And Shall These Mute Stones Speak?", was likely founded by the Irish-descended Dessi dynasty of Dyfed. We have seen above that fully *three* of the Irish Vortigerns hailed from the Dessi.

What can be said, with a fair degree of certainty, is that Fortchern son of Fedelmid (?) and the Irish Cunedda were contemporaries. Also, the son of Cunedda was buried in honor at the capital of Powys, Viroconium. Cunedda, his sons and their 'teulu' or war-band composed what the Saxons of southern England came to call the Gewessei.

According to Richard Coates (see his 'On some Controversy surrounding Gewissae/Gewissei, Cerdic and Ceawlin', NOMINA 13, 1989-90), Gewessei is "a nominalization of the [Old English] adjective gewis, among the meanings of which were 'sure, certain, reliable.'" These were federate warriors, the 'sure or reliable' ones. The Old English name nicely matches in meaning Latin fidus, from which comes foedus and then foederatus.

Cunedda and his teulu fought alongside Saxons against other British in the area. We can assume that as had been the case with Roman federates,

Cunedda and his followers were given lands in Gwynedd in return for rendering military service to the old Cornovii kingdom. Even if these lands had been granted in a de facto manner, a peaceful and supportive relationship could be sustained with Powys by the adoption of federate status. Doubtless this process had its origin in the Roman period.

Elafius, Elessa and Gewis

The identification of Elafius, an important man mentioned during the second mission of St. Germanus to Britain, with Elessa, father of Cerdic of Wessex, has long remained in doubt. Superficially, Elafius seems to be the Latin form of Greek Elafios, from elafos, "stag, hart". However, I believe there is good reason for upholding the Elafius-Elessa identification.

Many stories are generated by the false interpretation of proper and place-names. Elafius is said to have a lame son who was miraculously cured by St. Germanus. In this case, if we may allow for Constantius of Lyons, the 5th century author of the St. Germanus VITA, having a knowledge of Greek in addition to Latin, he may well have wrongly associated Gewis (archaic Giwis)*, the name of the father of Elessa in the Anglo-Saxon genealogies, with Greek GUIOS, "lame".

In the WELSH ANNALS, Gewis appears as Giuoys, in Asser as Geguuis and as Iwys, Iwis in ARMES PRYDEIN. Any of these forms may have reminded the author of the saint's VITA of the Greek word for lame. Although in the VITA it is

Elafius's son who is lame, not his father, as I have indicated in my previous discussion of the Ceawlin son of Cynric pedigree**, the actual order of birth at least for this pairing is Cynric son of Ceawlin (= the Cunorix son of Maquicoline found on an Irish memorial stone at Wroxeter). Thus at some point portions of the genealogy were reversed.

Granted, other words may have contributed to the lameness motif. Welsh has gloff, found as an epithet for a few early chieftains, while Latin has claudus, found in the Roman name Claudius. And Elessa has been plausibly linked to the Elisedd name found on the Elisedd Pillar at Llangollen. In my opinion, Elessa is from something comparable to Middle Welsh eilasaf, eiliasaf, adj. 'foremost, chief, most excellent, noblest, proudest, most generous'; n. 'leader, prince, chieftain'. This matches his description as 'regionis illus primus'. But whatever the original form of 'Elafius', I think a good case can be made for identifying his "lame" son with the Gewis of the Anglo-Saxon Chronicle and related sources.

A Note on the Grave of Vortigern

Robert Vermaat (see his award-winning Website Vortigern Studies) has elsewhere written about the Stanzas of the Graves which places Gwrtheyrn Gwrtheneu's 'doubtful' grave at an unlocated Ystyuacheu. To date, all efforts to locate this grave have failed. What follows is an attempt to both find this elusive burial site and to explore its significance in the broader context of just who Vortigern might have been.

The placename Ystyuacheu should be rendered in a more modern fashion as something like Styfacheu/Stafacheu/Stofacheu. Unfortunately, such a form is also not locatable. It is true, however, that MS. copyists frequently confused the letters u and n. This being so, I propose that perhaps the first -u- of Ystyuacheu might, in fact, have originally been an –n-. This would yield a Stynacheu/Stanacheu/Stonacheu.

In all of Wales, I found only one such Stynacheu/Stanacheu/Stonacheu site which made sense both etymologically and in terms of what we know of Vortigern. This is Stanage on the Teme River in Radnorshire. Stanage is from either OE stan + ecg, 'stone edge', or the ME stan + egge, with the same meaning.

The difference in the ending of Stanage and a hypothetical Stanageu/Stanagau may be accounted for in the same manner as the process by which the Cymracized English placename Stange became Stangau. These are the forms for Stange/Stangau:

STANGAU at SN761261 on map sheet SN72 900ft Parish of Llandeusant. 1948 OS 1:25000 First series.

STANGE 1840 OS 1" First edition (David & Charles reprint).

STANGAU 1891 OS6" First edition.

THE ARTHUR OF HISTORY

STANGE 1805-12 OS2" Original Drawing Map. RHIW alias STANGE 1808 Blaen Sawdde Estate Map. West Glamorgan Archives, Swansea.

As it turns out, Stange is a dialectal variant of stangau. The writers of some documents quite commonly 'corrected' the local pronunciation by inserting the standard form.

Stanage has a Welsh equivalent 'y Fron-faen' (modern spelling, 'the stone breast/steep hillside'). The English and Welsh versions seem to have existed side-by-side among the relative speech-communities for centuries, but the Welsh version seems to have disappeared around the end of the 16th century, as the Welsh language became extinct in the area.

At Stanage there is an early medieval motte, a medieval mound and bailey castle and medieval Stanage Castle. In my opinion, the motte was thought to represent the 'castle' in which Vortigern burned to death on the Teifi (according to Nennius). The question then becomes; 'Which tradition is correct' - that which places Vortigern on the Teifi or that which places him on the Teme?

To begin with, the similarity in the two river names could easily have led to confusion. The oldest forms of the Teme are of the type _Temede_ (which appears in Welsh as _Tefaidd_ (though the name now appears to be lost), while the earliest spellings for _Teifi_ are _Te(i)bi_, with an earlier form in Ptolemy (2nd century CE)

Touegobios or _Touerobios. Teifi and Teme are etymologically related; cf. Thames, in Welsh Tafwys. In terms of etymology, Teme and Teifi are linked because -f- is the result of lenition of earlier Welsh/British -m-.

The truly interesting thing about the Teme site is that it is, as already mentioned, located in Radnorshire. That portion of Radnorshire between the Wye and the Ithon rivers, which lies west of Stanage, was once known as the cantref of Gwrtheyrnion, i.e. the land of Vortigern. Stanage lies in Maelienydd cantref, which bordered on Gwrtheyrnion.

It would seem, therefore, that the original story had Vortigern dying on the Teme near Gwrtheyrnion. This site was transplanted to the Teifi to take advantage of the St. Garmon place-name found there. Geoffrey of Monmouth later moved the site once again, situating it at Ganarew near his home town.

The 'doubtful' quality assigned to Vortigern's grave at Stange is appropriate, as this king was almost certainly buried at Viroconium.

CHAPTER 2

ARTHUR'S ANCESTRY: RESTORING A GENEALOGY

For some time now I have been working on the "problem" of Uther Pendragon.

What is the nature of this problem, exactly? Simply this: 1) is Uther Pendragon, as it would appear to be, a name + epithet, or is it merely a title for another chieftain? And 2) how do we prove Uther actually was Arthur's father prior to Geoffrey of Monmouth?

No. 1 cannot really be answered with any certainty. There are other early British and Welsh names like Uther, "Terrible or Wondrous", i.e. names that have a distinctive adjectival quality. The formation itself, therefore, is not at all unique. Yet the combined effect of this supposed name + epithet IS unique, so far as I am aware. Other legitimate name + epithet pairings do not exhibit a linkage of meaning between the name and epithet. In other words, they cannot be read as a single title, as is the case with Uther Pendragon, the 'Terrible/Wondrous Chief-warrior'. Instead, the epithets are clearly separate descriptive modifiers of the names. This fact alone leads me to suspect that in Uther Pendragon we do have a title alone and not a name + epithet.

In the earliest sources, we have merely Arthur (see Nennius and the Welsh Annals). The Saints' Lives featuring Arthur also fail to name his father. There are a few references to Uther which have the appearance of being 'pre-Galfridian', i.e. before Geoffrey of Monmouth, but I will show here that we cannot always trust these references. Nor can we point to other Uthers in Welsh or Irish sources, as has sometimes been claimed.*

As an example of a poem which, on first glance, would appear to be pre-Galfridian, we may cite the Book of Taliesin's 'Kadeir Teyrnon'. Recently, Thomas Green tackled this poem, making some classic mistakes, precisely because he does approach the subject with the preconception that the material being treated of is pre-Galfridian ("A Note of Aladur, Alator and Arthur", STUDIA CELTICA, 41, 2007, 237-41).

Green identifies the aladwr of whom the 'Teyrnon' of the poem is said to be 'from the lineage of' with the obscure British god Alator, found in only two inscriptions. Although teyrnon by the 12th century had become a common noun meaning 'prince' and no longer was restricted to the divine personage Teyrnon of the Mabinogion, it is difficult to tell if the word here designates Arthur, who does appear with some prominence in the poem:

"The third profound [song] of the sage [is] to bless Arthur, Arthur the blest, with harmonious art; the defender of battle, the trampler on nine [enemies]."

There is a much more prosaic explanation for Arthur as 'echen aladwr', "of the family of

Aladwr". Arthur was of the family of the Breton Aldroenus, according to Geoffrey of Monmouth. In the Welsh genealogies, this Aldroenus becomes Aldwr. Uther's father Constantine/Custennin was the brother of this Aldwr. 'Aladwr' is thus merely a slight misspelling or corruption of Aldwr. Arthur is 'of the family of Al(a)dwr' and not of the god Alator.

The poem is thus immediately shown to NOT be pre-Galfridian. We must, therefore, be extremely cautious in how we approach this material. Especially as components from earlier Welsh tradition and from Geoffrey can be mixed in the same composition. In both the 'Uther Pen' and 'Chair of Teyrnon' poems there may be evidence of the inclusion of material from legendary saga. In one we learn of Cawrnur and in the other Gawr Nur, obviously the same personage. Cawr is Welsh for giant, while nur (from the GPC) appears to be a variant of nar or ner, 'lord, chief, leader', a word perhaps cognate with Irish nar/nair. This is likely the 'Bencawr' or Chief Giant Ysbyddaden ("Hawthorne"), who plays a pivotal role in the Welsh Arthurian story CULHWCH AND OLWEN. It should be noted that CULHWCH AND OLWEN does not appear to owe anything to Geoffrey.

Often cited by those who support the notion of a pre-Galfridian Uther is

1) The early Welsh poem 'Who is the porter?' In this poem we are told Mabon son of Modron (the Celtic god Maponos son of Matrona, identified by the Romans with their sun god Apollo) is the

guas or "servant" of Uthr Bendragon (see Chapter 6). No hint in the poem that this personage is Arthur's father.

2) Uthr Bendragon is mentioned in an early Triad (no. 28) as a great enchanter. Again, no mention is made of him being Arthur's father.

3) In two MSS. of Nennius a gloss after 'dux bellorum', used to describe Arthur, reads "In British Mab Uter, that is in Latin terrible son, because from his youth he was cruel." Here Arthur is not the son of Uther, but merely the 'Terrible Son'.

4) Madog son of Uthr is mentioned in the Book of Taliesin, and this same family connection is found in a didactic poem featuring Eliwlad son of Madog son of Uthr, were Arthur is specifically described as the uncle of Eliwlad. The poem is believed to have been composed in the middle of the 12th century, but survives only in a 15th century MS. A late Triad mentions this same Eliwlad son of Madog son of Uthr.

5) A Book of Taliesin poem entitled 'Marwnat Uthyr Pen' or 'Mar. Uthyr Dragon' mentions Arthur (although not as Uther's son).

Putting aside Nos. 3 and 4 for a moment, we need to look very carefully at No. 5. The attempt has been made (see, for example, most recently Thomas Green's "Concepts of Arthur"; I find the idea first broached in John Rhys's "Studies in the Arthurian Legend") to associate the Terrible (or Wondrous) Head of the 'Marwnat Uther Pen' with the head of Bran the Blessed. However, an epithet used in this poem – gorlassar, the origin of Geoffrey of Monmouth's Gorlois – is found used in only two other places in the early heroic poetry (see "The Poems of Taliesin", V.28, VIII.17). In both instances, THE WORD IS USED IN HONOR OF URIEN RHEGED.

In the poems of Llywarch Hen, we learn that upon Urien's death his head was cut off by Llywarch and born away in order to prevent it from coming into the possession of his enemies. This is quite remarkable, as the "Uthyr Pen" of the Taliesin poem can mean either "Terrible/Wondrous Head" OR (see the Geiriadur Prifysgol Cymru listing for pen) Terrible/Wondrous 'chief(tain), leader, lord, master, ruler'. Could it be that 'Uther Pen' is NOT Uther Pendragon, but is instead the head of the slain Urien Rheged?

Uther Pendragon, called gorlassar in a Taliesin poem (the origin of Geoffrey's 'Gorlois'), is Urien of Rheged, son of the Cynfarch (not Cynfor) who was the father of Eliffer's ("Constantine's") wife Efrddyl. I long suspected this, as gorlassar is otherwise found only in two places - and on both occasions it is used of Urien, once for his person and once for his spear. I resisted this conclusion for a long time because with Arthur as Urien's son I was forced not only to deal with the absence of Arthur in Cynfarch's line of descent, but also with a chronological impossibility: Urien is too late to be Arthur's father. Still, I can no longer deny that Urien of Rheged is Uther Pendragon.

The name may have come about as Uther Pen at first. I say this because in a Llywarch Hen poem, the hero bewails the fall of Urien and is in possession of his slain lord's head.

Professor John Koch once had a similar idea regarding the god Bran's severed head. Here is what he has to say in CELTIC CULTURE: A HISTORICAL ENCYCLOPEDIA:

"One possibility is that the strange and strangely named yspyddawt urddawl benn (feast of the stately head) around Brân's living severed head in the Mabinogi represents a garbling of a more appropriate 'feast of the uncanny head' (uthr benn); the marwnad would make sense as the words of the living-dead Brân mourning himself. For Geoffrey, the epithet Pendragon is 'dragon's head', an explanation of a celestial wonder by Merlin (see Myrddin). This meaning is not impossible..."

From Koch on the head of Urien:

"... another 30 lines describe Urien's decapitated corpse. In the former, there is much penetrating wordplay on the multiple senses of pen (head, chief, leader) and porthi (carry, support [e.g. of a poet by his patron]). The situation is reminiscent of that in Branwen, in which seven survivors, including the poet Taliesin, return from Ireland with the severed head of their king, Brân, and the englynion may intentionally echo this story:

Penn a borthaf ar vyn tu,

penn Uryen llary—llywei llu—
ac ar y vronn wenn vran ddu.

The head I carry at my side, head of generous Urien—he used to lead a host, and on his white breast (bron wen) a black crow (brân).

I would add that the 'Pa Gur' poem's phrase "Mabon son of Modron servant of Uther Pendragon" at last makes sense. For the center of Mabon worship, the locus Maponi of the Classical sources, was at the heart of Urien's kingdom in the North, and in the early poetry his son Owain is referred to as an incarnation of Mabon.

We should now look more closely at the gloss of the 'Uther Pen' poem. After receiving false or conflicting or just plain confusing information on this gloss from several sources, I finally asked Dr. Maredudd ap Huw, Manuscripts Librarian, Department of Collection Services at the National Library of Wales, to look at the MS. itself and let me know about the precise nature of this addition. The page in question can be viewed at: http://digidol.llgc.org.uk/METS/LLT00001/frames?div=78&subdiv=0&local...

Dr. Huw's response, in full:

"Firstly, I confirm that there is no ellipsis indicated in the manuscript, and that the gloss (or more correctly guide-title) reads 'mar. vthyr dragon.'

Secondly, on looking at the manuscript, it appears that the guide-title is written by the main scribe to inform the rubricator, who subsequently added the abbreviated title. The red ink of 'n' in 'pen' appears to cover the letter 'd' of 'dragon'.

I regret that I am not in a position to speculate as to why the rubricator did not follow the exact wording offered by the scribe in the guide-title."

This last is an important observation. The rubricator (called such because he used red ink) wrote 'marvnat vthyr pen.' for the main scribe's 'mar. vthyr dragon.' Why? The only explanation I can think of is that the rubricator supplied 'pen', with its meaning of chieftain, leader, lord, master, ruler, to explain the meaning of dragon in this context. In other words, he was aware that dragon could have two meanings. The first defined the mythological, reptilian monster of medieval legend. The second recorded its metaphorical use in heroic poetry.

We are not justified, therefore, is seeing a combined form epithet of Pendragon. Instead, the main scribe had only the 'Terrible/Wondrous Dragon', but with the meaning – as proven by the rubricator's addition to the MS. – of 'Terrible/Wondrous Chieftain'. The later construction 'Pendragon' would be a creation of Geoffrey of Monmouth or his reputed source. The original form of this name, if such it is, was merely 'Uther Dragon'.

This conclusion regarding the epithet Uther Pen/Dragon could negate the possibility that the poem's object is the decapitated head of Urien

Rheged. Or, even more likely, that a simple copying mistake was made.

No. 3 above, where Arthur is called 'mab Uter' or terrible son by a glossator in the 12th and 13th century Nennius MSS., is dispensed with as inconsequential.

If 'mab Uter' is being used this way with Arthur, then we are dealing with the only known usage of a mab + adjective phrase. If we could find examples of such usage in genuine early sources, we would have a precedent to go by. However, a 'mab X' formation always means "son of so-and-so", as far as we can tell. Yet support for such a reading as 'terrible son' – and for the notion that Uther Pendragon is merely a title for Arthur himself – seems to be found in Triad 1 and in 'Culhwch and Olwen", where Arthur referred to as 'Pen Teyrned', Chief Lord/Prince. It is not unreasonable to see in such a title a variant of Pen+ dragon.

But why would the glossator have added: "Mab Uter Britannice, id est filius horribilis Latine, quoniam a puritia sua crudelis fuit" or "In British Mab Uter, that is in Latin terrible son, because from his youth he was cruel"? We would expect instead for someone knowledgeable of the Galfridian tradition to tell us 'whose father is wrongly called Uter, mab Uter actually meaning that Arthur was a terrible son.' The reason is doubtless because the glossator is here attacking the Arthurian tradition. To this we may compare how poor Arthur is mercilessly beat up on in the Saints' Lives.

What the gloss plainly suggests is that the copyist had the name 'Arthur son of Uther', and knowing Uther was also an adjective meaning "horrible" or "terrible" (but also "wondrous"), he chose to interpret this as meaning Arthur was cruel from his youth. This is a fairly typical moralistic judgment applied by a Churchman to a civil ruler. It is meant to disparage the qualities of Arthur. To quote from THE NEW ARTHURIAN ENCYCLOPEDIA on the Saints' Lives in which Arthur appears:

"These stories disclose a discrepancy in Welsh clerical views of Arthur.... most of the Llancarfan matter presents him unfavorably. He is not an outright heathen, much less is he (as some have imagined) a demon in disguise... but he is a most unsatisfactory son of the Church and a troubler of the saints... Arthur is cast in the role of the Recalcitrant King, a stock character in this class of literature, who is brought in so that the saint can teach him a lesson through supernatural powers or superior virtue. His rapacity may be an echo of clashes between abbots and warrior chiefs... but nothing can be inferred about a real Arthur's real behavior."

In conclusion, such a gloss by a Churchman cannot be trusted to be an accurate reflection on the true nature of Uther.

And now for No. 4. The best source for the discussion of Madog or Madawg son of Uther is Patrick Sims-Williams' "The Early Welsh Arthurian Poems" (in THE ARTHUR OF THE WELSH,

1991). Here the fragment of the Book of Taliesin poem is rendered:

Madog, the rampart of rejoicing.

Madog, before he was in the grave,

He was a fortress of generosity

[consisting] of feat(s) and play.

The son of Uthr, before death [or 'before he was slain'],

He handed over pledges.

The author of the study readily admits that:

"Mab vthyr could mean 'terrible son/lad', but 'son of Uthr' is more likely, since Arthur's nephew is called the 'son of Madog son of Uthr' (mab madawc uab uthyr) in the "Dialogue of Arthur and the Eagle."

I agree with this assessment. It is true that the Madog stanza separates his name from the 'son of Uthr' by a few lines. We do not have here "Madog son of Uther". However, as I've said with the Nennius gloss 'mab uter', we have no precedent in the ancient poetry for a 'mab + adjective' formation. And the context of this poem presents Madog in a very favorable light, so that to refer to him as the 'terrible son' does not match the tone of the composition. In fact, such a description would be in direct opposition to everything else that is said in the poem about

Madog! There is absolutely nothing Galfridian about this poem fragment; Geoffrey does not know of a Madog son of Uther.

Sims-Williams states that "The Dialogue of Arthur and the Eagle" is extant only in fourteenth-century or later MSS., and that while it cannot be dated exactly, it may be as early as the twelfth century. That in and of itself is a problem, of course, as Geoffrey of Monmouth wrote his "History" in the 12th century. Its content may well have been influenced by Geoffrey of Monmouth. However, we must ask in what way it may have been thus influenced. As the poem fragment listing Madog son of Uther would appear to be genuine and in no way is dependent on Geoffrey, we can only say that the writer of the 'Dialogue', who knew of an Eliwlad son Madog son of Uther, may have been aware of the Galfridian tradition which made Arthur, too, a son of Uther.

The 'Dialogue' places Arthur in Cornwall, as was the Welsh belief at the time. As Sims-Williams indicates, the 'glyncoet Kernyw' of the poem is likely the large, wooded Glynn valley near Bodmin. I note here on maps a Cutmadoc Farm and Cutmadoc Newton. Cutmadoc does get a mention in Craig Weatherhill's "Place Names in Cornwall and Scilly" as Madoc's Wood (the prefix cut or cos appears all the time in Cornish place names and means small woodland). He also mentions an early 1320 form Coysmadok, but unfortunately doesn't give the source.

THE ARTHUR OF HISTORY

Gover's unpublished 1948 work on Cornish place names gives the following early forms: Codmadok and Cudmadek in 1302, Coysmadoc in 1314, Coysmadok in 1320, Cutmadok in 1327, Cosmadeck in 1547, and also says 'Cuit' is a Cornish language word for wood while 'Madoc' is a personal name.

Having covered the sources dealing with a supposed pre-Galfridian Uther, we must now treat of the epithet itself. In Geoffrey of Monmouth's account of the comet that appears on the death of Aurelius Ambrosius (the Ambrosius Aurelianus of Gildas), Merlin tells Uther that the dragon star signifies himself. This is NOT in accord with the prevailing medieval view. Simply expressed, a comet heralded the death of the king – something that Geoffrey does start out saying in his account. But such a star DID NOT represent, in any way, the dead king's successor.

Uther had nothing to do with the dragons of Dinas Emrys (a relocation of the Vespasian's Fort at Amesbury and nearby Stonehenge; see my book "The Mysteries of Avalon"). Beginning with the account of Emrys Guletic (Ambrosius the Prince) in Nennius, it is ONLY Aurelius who has to do with the dragons. In Geoffrey's History, Merlin is intruded and here wrongly identified with Ambrosius. Uther is placed in charge of obtaining the stones from Ireland with Merlin Ambrosius's help, but all this is done by order by Aurelius. In the original Dinas Emrys story it was Emrys/Ambrosius who revealed the dragons under the fort and who was then given the site to rule from by Vortigern. In fact, we are told Vortigern "gave him [Emrys] the fortress, with all the kingdoms of the western part of Britain." This is omitted, of course, when Geoffrey divides the Dinas Emrys episode from the Amesbury/Stonehenge one.

One more point is important here. According to Nennius (Chapter 31), Vortigern was in FEAR or DREAD (timore in the Latin text) of Ambrosius, who is called the "great king" (rex magnus) "among all the kings of the British nation". This title is a Latin rendering for his Welsh rank of guletic. In Welsh, uthr is an adjective and has the meanings of 'FEARFUL, DREADFUL' (see the Geiriadur Prifysgol Cymru). Thus the great king who was the terror of Vortigern could have become, quite naturally, the Terrible Dragon/Pen. Uther Dragon/Pen would then merely be a doublet for Ambrosius. This possibility may gain support from the fact that the late French Vulgate refers to Ambrosius as Pendragon.

Before anyone gets too excited about the notion that Uther Dragon, Arthur's father, is actually Ambrosius Aurelianus, I would remind everyone of the fact that Ambrosius himself has been anachronistically placed in the 5th century when he actually belongs in the 4th. He is the Roman governor of Gaul of this name; this explains why in Chapter 66 of Nennius, we are told that Ambrosius fights the GRANDFATHER of Vortigern at Wallop. A further confusion occurred when the historical meeting of St. Ambrose with Magnus Maximus/ (Welsh Macsen Guletic) at Aquileia was situated in story in Eryri ("abode of eagles") with Emrys Guletic (not here the historical Ambrosius, but the "Divine/Immortal One" Lleu, ruler of Gwynedd) and Vortigern

Various Arthurian researchers have sought to correct this anachronism by proposing the existence of a second Ambrosius Aurelianus, but unfortunately there is no justification for doing so. We would have to accept a descendent of the Gallic governor who was serving as leader of the Britons, or someone who had merely taken the name of the more famous Gallic leader. There is no evidence in support of either contention.

This gross anachronism, which took the 4th century Ambrosius Aurelianus and stuck him into the 5th century, is easy to explain. Gildas informs us that this hero's parents had "worn the purple". We know the Praetorian Prefect's exalted position was marked by his purple robe (see J.B. Bury's "History of the Later Roman Empire"). According to N. B. McLynn's "Ambrose of Milan: Church and Court in a Christian Capital" (1994):

"... [St.] Ambrose's homonymous father was praetorian prefect at the court of Constantine II, who ruled the western provinces from 337 until 340... the elder Ambrose died prematurely; the timing suggests a connexion with Constantine's disastrous invasion of the Italian territory of his brother Constans in 340 [the battle at which Constantine II died was fought at Aquileia]."

This Flavius Claudius Constantinus II and his brother Constans I are echoed by Flavius Claudius Constantinus III of 407-411 and his son, Constans II. Geoffrey of Monmouth makes both Ambrosius and Uther brothers of Constans II, son of Constantine III.

It has rightfully been objected to that a Praetorian Prefect of Gaul, who held a civil post, would not be fighting a battle anywhere – and certainly not in Britain. So how do we account for Ambrosius's placement at Wallop in Hampshire? Rather easily, as it happens. Ambrosius is placed at Wallop because of the latter's proximity to Amesbury, the earlier Ambresbyrig, only 10 or so miles to the WNW. Through the usual aetiological process, Amesbury was associated with Ambrosius's name. The great Danebury Hill fort overlooks the Wallop Brook. An even shorter distance separates Fittleton just to the north of Amesbury. This is Viteletone or "Fitela's tun" in the Domesday Book (and also a nearby Fitelan slad in 934). I have little doubt this place-name was wrongly brought into connection with the Latin Vitalinus.

In passing, I would mention the reference in the early Welsh poem "Gwarchan Maeldderw" (recently edited and translated by G. R. Isaac) to 'Pharaoh's Red Dragon'. This is a reference to the battle standard of the 'Fiery Pharaoh' (Welsh Ffaraon Ddande), a nickname for Vortigern derived from a passage in Gildas. We might be tempted to consider the possibility that Uther Dragon should instead be identified with Vortigern. But in truth, since Ambrosius supposedly took over the leadership of the Britons after Vortigern, and the Red Dragon is the genius of the British people, he would have inherited or wrested away the battle standard from his predecessor. We are here going by the traditional chronology, of course, which has Ambrosius follow Vortigern. The fort of Vortigern atop Dinas Emrys, with its red dragon, was "given" to Emrys by Vortigern.

The Uther Dragon/Uther Ben poem says "I have shared my refuge, a ninth share in Arthur's valour". If we assume the speaker is Arthur's presumed predecessor Ambrosius, then the statement is meant to imply that Ambrosius paved the way for his more glorious successor.

None of this, of course, actually pertains to Arthur's father, who must have been a different man. I will return to the quest for a real father for Arthur at the end of this chapter.

Two False Uthers

The Welsh Uther father of Cadolan found in Walter Map is not a legitimate Uther name, as is sometimes claimed (see p. 514, Rachel Bromwich's Trioedd Ynys Prydein: The Triads of the Island of Britain, 2014). It is instead a corruption of Ifor (Ibor) We know this because Cadolan is associated with a Gesligair, i.e. Gelligaer, so this is certainly Cadwallon son of Ifor who held the castle next to Gelligaer in the 12th century. Ibor is cognate with the Gaelic Iobhor/Iubor found as Arthur's father in the Scottish Campbell genealogy (although Ambros is also found as

Arthur's father in the Killbride version NLS MS 72). Curiously, the names Ibor/Iobhor/Iubor mean 'Yew'.

The Uthir/Uithir/Uithidir father of the Irish poet Adnae is merely an error for Uidhir (see under odor in the eDIL), a name meaning "of a dark or sallow complexion". It is unrelated to Welsh Uthr. In Irish, the cognate word for "terrible" is uath.

Geoffrey of Monmouth's Life of Uther

Geoffrey of Monmouth fleshed out the life of Uther, primarily by making use of episodes in the life of a 10th century Viking.

While this claim may seem outlandish, we need only go to the year entry 915 in the Anglo-Saxon Chronicle. There we are told of the Jarls Ohtor and Hroald or Hraold, who come from Brittany to raid the Welsh coast along the Severn Estuary. They concentrate their initial attacks on Archenfield, the Ercing where Aurelius and Uther are first placed when they come to England from Brittany. Hroald is slain by the men of Hereford and Gloucester, but Ohtor goes on to land 'east of Watchet'. The Willet or 'Guellit' River, adjacent to Carhampton, the ancient Carrum, is east of Watchet. Both the Willet and Carhampton feature in the tale of Arthur and the terrible dragon ('serpentem ualidissimum, ingentem, terribilem') in the 11th century Life of St. Carannog or Carantog. I would propose that this terrible dragon owes its existence to the dragon-ship of Ohtor, i.e. a typical Viking ship with a dragon's head at its prow and a dragon's tail at its stern, and that Geoffrey of Monmouth made use of the terrible dragon's presence at Carrum to associate Uther with Ohtor. After an unpleasant stay on an island (Steepholme or Flatholme), Ohtor and what remains of his host go to Dyfed, where Uther is said to fight Pascent and the Irish king Gillomanius. Ohtor then proceeds to Ireland, where Uther had previously fought Gillomanius over the stones of Uisneach/Mount Killaraus.

We have, then, the following startling correspondences:

Uther in Brittany	Ohtor in Brittany
Ercing	Archenfield
Carrum (terrible dragon)	East of Watchet
Menevia in Dyfed	Dyfed
Ireland	Ireland

This Viking jarl is found in the Welsh Annals under the year 913, where the concise entry reads 'Otter came'. This reference to Ottar is also found in the Welsh Brut t tywysogion (Chronicle of the Princes).

Mount Damen: The Lost Battle of Uther Pendragon

In Geoffrey of Monmouth's "History of the Kings of Britain", we are told that when Uther Pendragon is defeated by the Saxons at York, he and his army retreat to a Mount [or hill of] Damen. Here they take refuge, attacking and destroying the Saxon camp in a bold night-time attack that is the brain-child of Gorlois. Following this victory, Uther travels to Alclud in Scotland to pacify that region.

Various candidates have been sought for Mount Damen, an otherwise unlocated place-name. Rather early on Damems near Bradford in West Yorkshire was proposed. Unfortunately, as Dr. Paul Cavill of the English Place-Name Society has assured me, Damems is from ON dammr + ME ende, attested first in 1620. This site is also not on any of the main roads of the time. I once thought to connect Damen with either the Dauen- of Daventry (Dauen- being the genitive of the personl name Dafi) or even with the name of the Dane stream (Dauen) on the other side of the Pennines from York. But these places are too far away, as Uther supposedly retreated to Damen in less than a day.

We have a number of important clues in Geoffrey's account that help us pinpoint Mount Damen. First, he tells us that Uther appointed as bishop of Alclud one Eledenius. As P.C. Bartrum noted, this is the St. Elidan that is known from churches in the Vale of Clwyd. Therefore, Geoffrey's Alclud is an error for Clwyd. The most direct route from York to Chester and thence to Clwyd ran through Huddersfield (with its Roman camp of Cambodunum at Slack), up and over Standedge ridge on the Pennines pass, down to Castleshaw (with its Roman camp of Rigodunum), to Manchester, etc.

The name Huddersfield – once one comes to know how Geoffrey operates – is vitally important in our quest for Damen. As I've shown

THE ARTHUR OF HISTORY

in my book THE SECRETS OF AVALON, much of Uther's career was "padded out" by associating him with a Viking chieftain named Jarl Ohtor. The same process may have been at work on a folkloristic level at Pendragon Castle in Cumbria, where Outgill (from a Scandinavian audr + gill) may have falsely suggested Uther's presence. So, a perceived similarity in names was important to Geoffrey when he was composing his tale. The early forms (Domesday Book) of Huddersfield (see Ekwall and Mills) are Odresfelt or Oderesfeld, from either a man named *Hudraed or OE "huder, 'a shelter' (both unattested, postulated names/words). These forms set off alarm bells and I begin to delve into the history and topography of Huddersfield more closely.

Armitage Goodall ("Place-Names of South-west Yorkshire, 1914), has:

"In DB we find Oderesfelt, Pdersfelt, Odresfeld, but later spellings are of a different character and should ge compared with those of Hothersall near Preston... The DB forms of Huddersfield are obvisouly at fault: they omit the aspirate as in Arduuic of Hardwick, and they give o for u as in Podechesaie for Pudsey, defects both due to Norman scribes... on the lips of the man in the street Huddersfield is sometimes 'Uthersfield'; compare SM 1610 Huthersfield, RE 1634 Hothersfield."

The "Publications of the University of Manchester" (1922) comments on the place-name Hothersall thusly:

"The first el. of the name is no doubtr a pers. n., identical with that in Huddersfield... But it is not easy to explain such a name. The O.E. Huthhere (~Hythhere) does not account well for the regular d of the early forms."

According to 'A Castle Well Guarded': the Archaeology and History of Castle Hill, Almondbury' by John Rumsby, in E A Hilary Haigh (ed), Huddersfield: A Most Handome Town (Huddersfield, 1992),

"Medieval documents mention a piece of land near or on the hill, call 'Wormcliffe'. This name probably derives from the Anglo-Saxon 'wyrm', meaning a dragon."

George Redmonds' "Place-Names of Almonbury" adds more on this Wormcliff designation for Castle Hill:

"... it does seem likely that the hill retained a sinister reputation among the English, who called it Wormeclyff. This was first recorded in the rental of 1425 as the name of certain demesne lands on the "hill where the castle used to stand": later, in the Minster's Accounts of 1487, it was more precisely indentified as "the castle of Wormecliff"... The word 'cliff' was formerly used for any steep bank, not just a precipice, and it clearly refers to Castle Hill itself, or some portion of it. More signifiant is the word 'worm' which for the English meant a serpent or even a dragon, a fearful creature haunting old ruins or guarding lost treasure."

THE ARTHUR OF HISTORY

Thus there may once have been a story of a dragon at Almondbury.

The Roman camp at Slack took its name from the nearby Brigantian hill-fort, now called Almondbury or Castle Hill. However, at some point in the 12th century (bear in mind Geoffrey completed his "History" in 1136), the de Lacy family, who had owned Almondbury since prior to the death of Ilbert de Lacy in 1089, built a castle there. Lacy is from Lassy in Calvados.

The Lassy name set off another alarm. Why was it that Gorlois (from the epithet gorlassar found used of Uther Pendragon in 'Marwnat Vthyr Pen[dragon]') is first mentioned at the Mount Damen battle? I could not help but see Geoffrey assuming that Gor- was the usual Welsh intensive prefix, leaving –lois to imaginatively relate to Lassy/Lacy.

Or was all of this merely fanciful on my part? Everything depended on how we derive the place-name Damen.

Best bet? Damen is for the common Welsh word tomen or domen, meaning 'hillock, mound', but also '[castle] motte'. If I am right with this etymology, then the 'hill of the motte' would simply be a designation for Almondbury's de Lacy motte at 'Odresfelt'.

The geography, the presence of the Roman road, etc., all point to this being a reasonable identification for Mount Damen. Uther is to be imagined as retreating from York along the main

Roman road that ran to Chester. He reaches Huddersfield/Odresfelt, where his army takes refuge atop the motte or tomen/domen/'Damen' of Almondbury. There Gorlois, because the motte was Lassy/Lacy, first makes his appearance and promotes the idea of the nocturnal attack on the Saxons. Once the Saxons have been defeated, Uther proceeds to Clwyd, where he subjugates this part of Wales, placing over it 'Bishop'/Saint Elidan.

Some support is added to my argument for Huddersfield by the fact that Ambrosius had previously fought at Ballifield near Sheffield (Geoffrey's Maisbeli; see Mark English's article at http://nq.oxfordjournals.org/content/61/1/11.short?rss=1) and Conisborough. Both of these sites are in the same general region as Huddersfield.

So Who Is Arthur's Real Father?

We have seen above that it is possible Uther Dragon or Uther Pendragon may be a title for the chronologically and geographically misplaced Ambrosius Aurelianus.
Given this possibility, as well as Uther's life having been based upon the career of a Viking and the aetiological use of place-names, we are left with no obvious father for the 5th-6th century Arthur. Or is this necessarily true?

Already considered as a candidate was the chieftain Urien of Rheged. Uther Pen may refer to the head of Urien, carried about by Llyward Hen after his death. The use of the epithet gorlassar for

Uther Pen also pointed to Urien. Unfortunately, the date for Urien is too late for him to be Arthur's father. But could he still be related to Arthur somehow?

In the traditional genealogies for Arthur, Cynfawr (= Cunomorus) or Cynfarch is made the father of Custenin/Constantine the father of Uther. Urien is son of Cynfarch son of Meirchiaun.

In the Welsh genealogies we encounter a chieftain of the North named Eliffer Gosgorddfawr (Eleutherius of the Great Retinue). Eliffer's epithet is significant. This 'great retinue' may be a memory either of the Sixth Legion, which was stationed at York, or of a comitatensis.

Eliffer's real father is thought to have been one ARTHWYS (although see Chapter 5 and Appendix II for this personal name as a possible territorial designation) and he had a son named Peredur, the Welsh form of the Roman rank of Praetor (hence the later Peredur son of Ebrauc, the latter being an eponym for the city of Eboracum/York, headquarters of the Roman praetor). During the Roman period, the governor of Northern Britain at York was a Praetor, or to be more specific, a Praetorian Prefect. I do not hold to the idea that Peredur is instead from *Pritorix, the handsome king, fair-shaped king (see Rachel Bromwich's Triads of the Island of Britain, p. 561).

Eleutherius is a Greek name, and these were popular in northern Europe in the 5th century.

It means "Liberator", and this is certainly significant.

Why? Because York is famous for its association with Constantine the Great, who not only declared himself emperor while at the city, but went out of his way to present himself as the Liberator of Rome and, indeed, of the world (see laweb.usc.edu/centers/clhc/events/feature/documents/Lenski_ConstantineUSC.pdf). Greek writers, of course, when speaking of him as the Liberator used words derived from eleutheros/eleutheria.

I would surmise that a sort of "cult" of Constantine the Great might have existed in 5th century York and that Eleutherius as a name was actually originally derived from Constantine's Liberator title. [The 'The Twenty-Four Mightiest Kings', Custennin Fendigaid, i.e. the Welsh version of Geoffrey of Monmouth's Constantine III, is called Waredwr, 'the Deliverer'. This suggests that Constantine III was here confused with the earlier Constantine the Liberator.]

Eliffer's sons Peredur and Gwrgi are recorded as fighting at a place called Caer Greu ('Fort Greu') and at Arfderydd/Arthuret just NW of Carlisle. Greu has been tentatively related to W. creu, 'blood'. I would propose that Caer Greu/Creu is Carrawburgh, i.e. the Roman fort of Brocolitia, on Hadrian's Wall. English 'Carrawburgh' could easily reflect something like very early Old Welsh *'Cair Carrou'. The extant form of 'Caer Greu' could be the regular Middle Welsh reflex of this. Carrawburgh is not far from Corbridge, where

THE ARTHUR OF HISTORY

Arthur's Dubglas River battles were fought (see Chapter 3).

Their presence at Arthuret shows that they were active in the same area as Arthur, who died in battle at Castlesteads/Camboglanna on the Wall not far to the east (see again Chapter 3).

Eliffer's wife Efrddyl, daughter of Cynfarch son of Merchiaun, is said to have had three children: Gwrgi, Peredur and either Ceindrech or Arddun Benasgell (sometimes called 'Wing-head'; however, as asgell can also mean 'spear' or even 'wing of an army', her epithet may mean instead either 'Spear-head', a reference to her weapon, or 'Spear-chieftain', or even 'Chieftain of the Army Wing'). Arddun is elsewhere said to be the daughter of Pabo Post Prydyn. But in the slightly corrupt Jesus College MS. 20, Arddun's name is replaced by ARTHUR PENUCHEL.

Rachel Bromwich discussed this supposed corruption in her revised edition of 'The Triads of the Island of Britain", and I am quoting her here in full:

"Ardun Pen Askell is probably the correct form of the name of the sister of Gwrgi and Peredur... But if is likely that it is this name which has been corrupted to arthur penuchel in Jes. Gens. 20... The manuscript is of the turn of the 14th/15th century, but with indications of having been copied from an earlier exemplar... These points suggest that the triad may be as old as any that hav been preserved in the earlier collections... And in fact the context in which the triad is cited in Jes. Gens. 20 points to the probable source which inspired its composition This is the allusion to the progeny of Nefyn daughter of Brychan which is contained in the tract De Situ Brecheniauc, preserved in a thirteenth century manuscript, which has been copied from one of perhaps the eleventh century."

We should pay a bit more attention to this alteration.

Why? Firstly, although it has been customary to view the alteration as a corruption, we cannot be sure that this is so in this particular context. It could represent, in fact, a CORRECTION or even a SUBSTITUTION.

Or an ADDITION: in 'The Dialogue of Myrddin and Taliesin", we are told of the "seven sons of Eliffer." While this may be mere poetic rhetoric, the possibility that Eliffer had sons in addition to Peredur and Gwrgi leaves for an Arthur among them.

The truly remarkable thing about this "corruption" of Arthur Penuchel is that it is found attached to the royal house of York – the one place we know of that had seen a Roman period camp prefect named Artorius, and the one place where the name may have been remembered by Britons claiming Romano-British descent. This is simply too big of a coincidence, in this author's opinion. Of all the other lines of descent for the Men of the North the name could have been attached to, it was attached only to the family of Eliffer/Eleutherius.

Only recently, while taking another look at Arthur's claimed connections with Ercing in SE Wales (most or all the product of folklore and Geoffrey of Monmouth's imagination), I noticed a second Efrddyl. She was the daughter of King Peibio of Ercing and mother of St. Dubricius. More importantly, her own mother *was a daughter of a king named Constantinus.*

A Constantine was given a daughter by Anblaud of Ercing, and their son was Goreu. This same Anblaud was the father of Eigr, wife of Uther and mother of Arthur.

So, we are up to our gills in Constantines!

To make matters worse, the names/titles Anblaud Wledig and Uther Pendragon are near perfect matches for each other. Anblaud the 'very terrible/fearful' appears to be a made-up name, a sort of play of words, with his kingdom of Ercing being related to W. erch, "terrible, frightful." Brynley F. Roberts long ago stated his belief that Anblaud was a fictional kingdom-founding ancestor for Arthur and his extended family relations.

What we may have then, is this: a southern pedigree running Cynfarch-Constantine-Uther-Arthur and a northern one that is very similar, but relies upon the maternal line, i.e. Cynfarch, brother of Urien/Uther Pen- Efrddyl daughter of

Cynfarch, brother of Urien and wife of Eleutherius/"Constantine"-Arthur.

The Arthwys preferred as the father of Eliffer displays the Celtic arth, 'bear', component and the Welsh interpreted the Arth- of Arthur in the same way. Recently, the Roman name Artorius as been etymologized as deriving ultimately from the Celtic, meaning "Bear-king" (see Stefan Zimmer's "The Name of Arthur – A New Etymology", Journal of Celtic Linguistics, 13, 2009, 131-6; there, Artorius is shown to be from Celtic *Arto-rig-ios, 'Bear-king'). If the arth/'bear' component was already in Arthwys's family, then it is not unreasonable to suppose that his grandson also bore this component as part of his own name. The name Arthur is indisputably from the Roman Artorius.

Penuchel, the epithet assigned to this Arthur, is given a couple different meanings. Patrick K. Ford of Harvard, translator of the Mabinogion, rendered Penuchel (in the context of Sawyl Penuchel of Samlesbury hard by Ribchester) as 'Overlord'. The GPC dictionary, on the other hand, reading it as 'high-head', gives it a transferred sense of 'haughty, arrogant'. 'Overlord' would fit the context better, as this would be a good description of the role Arthur is said to have played in the 'Historia Brittonum' of Nennius. When I wrote to Professor Ford and asked him why he had chosen the rendering 'Overlord', he replied:

"The answer is a choice based on context and the semantic fields of penn and uchel."

THE ARTHUR OF HISTORY

It should be stressed that Penuchel as an epithet for Sawyl of Ribchester is a later replacement for an earlier Penisel, 'low-head' or 'the humble' – perhaps better, 'under-lord'.

Granted, the established chronology for the Eliffer dynasty does not exactly support my contention that Arthur of the North was a son of Eliffer. Obviously, Arthur was not a contemporary of Urien! But Arthur may have been born to Eliffer and Efrddyl very early on, while their sons Gwrci and Peredur were produced years later.

Finally, the chronologies that have been worked out for these early Men of the North are rough approximations and thus cannot be relied upon for any kind of precise dating. I will discuss below the very real possibility that Arthur was not a son of Eliffer, but instead his brother.

The Dalriadan Connection

At this point in our exploration of Arthur's real parentage, we must pause to consider the implications of the intrusion of the founder of the Scottish Dalriadan dynasty into the early British pedigrees. For sources on the following details, please see P.C. Bartram's relevant works.

I've already mentioned that Arthwys was the father of Eliffer – but this is so only in the PREFERRED genealogy. Preferred primarily for the purposes of establishing a reasonable chronology, that is. But an early version of Eliffer's pedigree lists Gwrwst Ledlwm as his father. Because this Gwrwst is said to have had a son name Dyfnarth, P. K. Johnstone long ago suggested that Dyfnarth was, in fact, Domangart, son of Fergus Mor of Dalriada. I agree with his assessment, and for good reason: Arthwys's father is said to be one Mar, whose name is spelled Mor in later versions of the pedigree. Early Irish used Mar and Mor interchangeably.

In other words, Mar/Mor = Fergus Mor = Gwrwst Ledlwm. [Mor is 'great' in Irish, but the cognate word in Welsh was mawr. Mor in Welsh means 'sea'.]

Mar is also made the father of Lleenog, father of Gwallog of Elmet. But a conflicting genealogy claims that Lleenog's father was one Maeswig. Mar (and his son Arthwys) are also thrust into the pedigree of Pabo Post Prydyn, otherwise the son of Ceneu.

Arthur of Dalriada is made variously the son of Aedan or of his son, Conaing (the latter name being a borrowing of English cyning, 'king', and so merely a confused reference to Aedan himself as King of Dalriada?). This Dalriadan Arthur was named after his more famous predecessor, who according to a corrupt source may have been a son of Eliffer of York (although see below for Arthur as a brother of Eliffer).

Why Was Arthur's Parentage Forgotten?

It was only natural for Arthur to become attached to Ambrosius as Uther Pendragon, for other than Arthur, Ambrosius – though a fiction transplanted from Gaul - was the most famous commander of the period. The process was undoubtedly made easier by the supposed Constantine connection, something that became attached to Dumnonia in the southwest of England precisely because the royal house there had as its semi-legendary progenitor Geraint, himself patterned after Gerontius, the British magister militum of Constantine III. York, too, had its "cult of Constantine (the Great)." Thus it was not difficult to transfer Arthur from the region of York to that of Dumnonia.

But none of this explains why Arthur's real father's name was forgotten. As it turns out, I believe this may have happened precisely because Arthur himself went by another name.

The personage we will be considering was not a son of Eliffer of York, but actually his brother.

Arthur Dux Bellorum and Ceidio son of Arthwys

There has always been a problem with the 'dux bellorum' title applied to the legendary Arthur.

To begin, there is a misconception that the so-called title actually appears this way in the text of Nennius's Latin HISTORIA BRITTONUM. In fact, it does not. The text actually reads 'sed ipse dux erat bellorum', 'but he himself was leader of battles'. As has been discussed before by experts in early Medieval Latin who have studied Nennius, this is NOT a title. It cannot be equated, therefore, with the dux legionum rank of the third century Roman Lucius Artorius Castus, who led a single campaign against the Armenians. It certainly can't be compared with the same man's rank of praefectus (castrorum) of the Sixth Legion at York. For a good discussion of the ranks held by LAC, see http://www.christophergwinn.com/celticstudies/lac/lac.html.

This description applied to Arthur in the HB seems to have led to him being referred to in subsequent sources as simply a miles or 'soldier.' The idea has often been floated that this means Arthur was not a king and, in fact, may not even have been of royal blood. Truth is, Arthur may not have been king – if he predeceased his father, for instance. We do not have to resort to the 2nd-3rd century Roman soldier Lucius Artorius Castus to account for the 5th-6th century chieftain being considered only a 'leader of battles.'

But if not a title, could this Latin phrase have designated a secondary, purely British name belonging to Arthur?

Myself and others have pointed out that attested early names such as Cadwaladr, ("Catuwalatros) 'Battle-leader', Caderyn (Catutigernos), 'Battle-lord', Cadfael (Catu-maglos), 'Battle-prince', Caturix (a Gaulish god), 'Battle-king', could have yielded a description such as 'dux erat bellorum'. No names of this nature appear to have been known in the North (where I've shown Arthur to belong) during the Arthurian period.

However, it has recently occurred to me that my tentative genealogical trace of Arthur to Arthwys, the latter being a name or a regional designation of the valley of the River Irthing on the western part of Hadrian's Wall, may hold the clue to unraveling the dux bellorum mystery. Arthur died at Camboglanna/Castlesteads on the Cambeck, a tributary of the Irthing.

The son of Arthwys in the genealogies is given as Ceidio, born c. 490 (according to P.C. Bartram), quite possibly the same chieftain whose son is mentioned in the ancient Gododdin poem as 'mab Keidyaw'. John Koch and others have discussed Ceidio as a by-form of a longer two element name beginning with *Catu-/Cad-, 'Battle'.

Dr. Simon Rodway was kind enough to write the following to me on Ceidio:

"Ceidiaw is a 'pet' form of a name in *katu- 'ba tle' with the common hypocoristic ending -iaw (> Mod. Welsh -(i)o) found in Teilo (Old Welsh Teliau) etc., and still productive today (Jaco, Ianto etc.). And yes, it's not possible to say what the second element would have been. But the forms you suggest [Cadwaladr, Cateryn] are among the candidates, especially as this man was a chieftain of Y Gogledd [the North] at the head of some of the royal genealogies. "

In other words, this Ceidio would originally have had a full-name of the type Cadwaladr or Cateryrn. Unfortunately, we can never know what the second "dropped" element of his name might originally have been. However, if Roman naming practices had been preserved in the North during Arthur's time, we would reasonably expect a form such as X Artorius Z, where X, the praenomen, was the given name, Artorius was the nomen, i.e. gens or clan name, and Z was the cognomen, i.e. the name of the family line within the gens. A Cad- name, shortened to Ceidio, might well have been one of Arthur's other names.

Of course, by the time of the 5th-6th centuries, the Roman gens name Artorius may well have been given to a prince as his praenomen. If the name had retained its status as a gens name, then that would mean someone in the Irthing River region actually traced his descent from Lucius Artorius Castus. While this could be either a genuine or fabricated trace, it is also possible the name was remembered as belonging to a famous figure of legend and passed on to a favorite son for that reason alone.

In the contents description of the Harleian recension of Nennius, we find the phrase 'Arturo rege belligero', something usually translated as "King Arthur the warrior". More accurately, this is 'Arthur the warlike or martial king'. Suppose we allow for rege belligero as an attempt at a literal Latin rendering of something like Cadwaladr or Cateryn?

The fifth century St. Patrick, who I've shown came from the Banna fort on Hadrian's Wall at modern Birdoswald on the Irthing, is known to have had a typical Roman style 'three-part' name: Patricius Magonus Sucatus. Patricius is believed to have been his Christian name, assumed after his conversion, but it is just as possible he bore a classic Roman-structured name from birth.

If I'm right about Arthur being a son of Arthwys – or being FROM Arthwys – and we can allow for Ceidio son of Arthwys having originally born a name like Cadwaladr or Cateryn, then it is not inconceivable that Arthur DOES appear in the Northern genealogies after all.

Arthur and Ceidio would be one and the same man.

It has occurred to me that if Arthwys was a real name or even a geographical entity, and he belonged specifically in the Irthing Valley, and Ceidio son of Arthwys's son Gwenddolau (or 'White Dales') belonged at Carwinley, then Ceidio himself might have held a region or fort between these two locations.

In this book I discuss Stanwix near Carlisle. Etterby hard by Stanwix was once known as 'Arthur's burg [or fort].' However, as it turns out (see below), Etterby was surely a mistake for Stanwix itself, site of the largest cavalry force in all of Britain and the command center for much of Hadrian's Wall.

The Roman name for Stanwix was Uxellodunum, the 'High Fort.' British uxello- becomes in Welsh uchel - the exact same word we find in that Penuchel epithet applied to Arthur son of Eliffer.

Could it be that Penuchel means the 'Chief of Uchel[-dunum]'?

Stanwix was also called after the unit that garrisoned the fort, the Ala Petriana (named for Pomponius *Petra*). This reminds us of the fact that the later Arthur of Dyfed was the son of one *Petr*.

These ideas are, admittedly, far-fetched, and I would warn against placing any emphasis upon them. Still, they are in interesting and, perhaps, worth mentioning in passing.

CHAPTER 3

THE BATTLES OF ARTHUR

The First Battle: The Mouth of the River Glein

It has long been recognized that there are only two extant Glen rivers which conform philologically to 'Glein' and which could have been subject to Saxon attack from the Continent in the 5th-6th centuries CE, the Age of Arthur.

These are the Glen of Lincolnshire and the Glen tributary of the Till in Northumberland.

The Glen of Lincolnshire has no distinctive features or strategic fortifications which would make it of any value to an invading force. On the other hand, the Northumberland Glen is hard by the Yeavering Bell hill-fort, which prior to becoming a Saxon stronghold was the British Gefrin. Gefrin is from the Welsh word gafr 'goat' or a compound containing gafr plus Welsh bryn (mutated fryn), for 'Goat-hill'. I would remind the reader, however, of a Gaulish god conflated with Mercury called Gebrinius. It is possible that Gefrin represents a British counterpart of this divine name.

The Yeavering Bell hillfort is 12.8 acres in size and encloses the two summits and the saddle between of a hill that rises to a height of 1181 ft above sea level. There is a single stone rampart

13 ft wide, with entrances midway along the north and south sides, and a third on the northeast.

At the east and west ends are small, crescent-shaped annexes, the latter with an entrance at its mid-point. The centre of the fort was the site of about 130 circular huts. The eastern summit is ringed by a trench which held a wooden palisade nearly 164 ft in diameter. Archaeologists do not know whether there is any relationship between the hillfort and the Anglo- Saxon royal town of Ad Gefrin ('at Gefrin') that succeeded it at the foot of the hill.

Other hill-forts abound in the region: Wooler, Kyloe Hills, Dod Law forts at Doddington, the Old Bewick hill fort and the Ros Castle fort and settlement between Chillingham and Hepburn. And, of course, the Roman road known as the Devil's Causeway, a branch off of Dere Street, passes only a couple of miles to the east of the mouth of the Glen.

Scholars who argue in favor of the Lincolnshire or 'Lindsey' Glen do so primarily because the following battle, that of the Dubglas, is put in a Linnuis region by the HB. Linnuis, as we will see, is wrongly thought to represent the later regional name Lindsey.

An actual battle at the mouth of the Lindsey or Lincolnshire Glen is scarcely possible, unless it were a battle of reconquest by Arthur and not a successful defensive engagement. This is because we have archaeological evidence for Saxon cemetaries well north, west and south of the Lindsey Glen as early as c. 475 CE.

The Next Four Battles: The River Dubglas in the Linnuis Region

Philologists have long recognized that Old Welsh Linnuis must derive from Br.-Lat. *Lindensis, *Lindenses, or *Lindensia, and the identification with Lindsey works fine on purely linguistic grounds. Lindsey, of course, was the early English name for what we now think of as Lincolnshire.

The root of Lindensis is British *lindo-, 'pool, lake', now represented by Welsh llyn, 'pond, lake'. The Roman name for the town of Lincoln – Lindum – is from the same root. The 'pool' or 'lake' in question is believed to have been on the Witham River near the town.

The problem is that there is no Dubglas or 'Black Stream' (variants Douglas, Dawlish, Dowlish, Divelish, Devil's Brook, Dalch, Dulais, Dulas, etc.) in Lindsey. This has caused other place-name experts to situate the Dubglas battle either near Ptolemy's Lindum of Loch Lomond in Scotland or near Ilchester in Somerset, the Roman period Lindinis, as there are Dubglas rivers in both places. We might even look to the Douglas River in Lancashire, not far west of the Roman Ribchester fort. Unfortunately, none of these candidates is satisfactory, because Arthur would not have been fighting Saxons at these locations in the time period we are considering.

A site which has been overlooked, and which is an excellent candidate for Arthur's Dubglas, is the Devil's Water hard by the Hadrian's Wall fort of Corbridge, which has upon it a place called Linnels. Almost a century ago it was proposed that Linnels was from an unrecorded personal name. But modern place-name expert Richard Coates, upon looking at Linnels on the Ordnance Survey map, observed the remarkable double elbow in the Devil's Water with a lake nearby and concluded that Linnels was from a British *lindo-ol:in, "lake-elbow".

It was once thought that the Devil's Water stemmed from a Dilston Norman family, the D'Eivilles. But going by the earliest spelling of the Devil's Water (Divelis c. 1230) leads recent authorities to state uncategorically that this etymology is incorrect and the Devil's Water is certainly of the Dubglas river-name type.

The Devil's Water at Linnels is thus the only extant Dubglas river-name associated with a demonstrably Welsh lake-name that is geographically plausible as a battle site against Britons and Saxons during the period of Arthur. Worth noting is the fact that the Roman Dere Street road at Corbridge splits immediately north of the Wall, the eastern branch or 'Devil's Causeway' continuing North-NorthEast, straight to the Northumberland Glen.

As an aside, I would mention that the Battle of Hexham was fought at Linnels on May 14, 1464.

The Sixth Battle: The River Bassas

THE ARTHUR OF HISTORY

The Bassas river is the most problematic of the Arthurian battle sites, as no such stream name survives and we have no record other than this single instance in the HB of there ever having been a river so named. We can only say that the location of the Bassas may be somewhere in the same general region as the Glen and Devil's Water battles. We will see below that the locations of subsequent battle sites will support this notion.

Some Arthurian theorists have opted for very questionable identications of Bassas. They have pointed to Bass place names such as Bass Rock in the Firth of Forth, the Bass at Inverurie in Aberdeenshire and Bass Hill at Dryburgh.

Alas, the etymology for bass is fairly recent. In the Scottish National Dictionary there is an entry under 'bass' as follows: "A workman's tool basket; also a basket for carrying fish – known in Banff and Fife: on Lothian coast 'bass' is a square straw basket about 2' by 2' used for ca rying fish."

Bass Rock and similar formations would have been named by fisher folk due to their resemblance to such a basket.

The Bass Burn or Bass 'stream', a tributary of the Scar or Scaur Water approximately 15 miles North-West of Dumfries and just south of Auchenhessnane, was originally called the Back Burn. Both the 1st edition (1861) and 2nd edition (1899) Ordnance Survey maps name it as

Back Burn. The 1955 edition names it as Bass Burn. It is possible that either the original surveyors simply misheard what the local people called it, or that later surveyors did. As there are other Back Burns in Lowland Scotland, the chances that this stream's original name was Bass is slim.

An acceptable, and perhaps preferable, explanation for the name Bassas is that it records an OE personal name found in place-names, i.e. Bassa. This is the view of Graham Issac.

The ending -as in Bassas would appear to have no explanation in either Latin or Welsh grammar. But it does have an explanation in Old English grammar. The name could thus be Old English. Just as Baschurch (Shropshire) is from Old English 'Basses cirice', i.e. 'Basse's church' (Eglwyseu Bassa in the Old Welsh poems), and Basford (Nottinghamshire) is Old English 'Basses ford', and Baslow Derbyshire) is Old English 'Basses hlaw', i.e. 'Basse's burial-mound'; so 'flumen quod uocatur Bassas' is easily unde stood as 'the river which is called Basse's', i.e. 'Basse's river'. There is a Basingbourne in Cambridgeshire, Old English Basingeburna, which is 'the stream of Basse's people', 'Basse's kin's stream'.

There are two genuine OE Bassa place-names further north in Northumberland. Bassington in Cramlington parish was a farmstead a litte over a mile north-west of the village. It appears on a map of 1769 and is probably a much older site. In the present day town of Cramlington the site of Bassington Farm is on the Bassington Industrial Estate. However, other than this Bassington's proximity to the Devil's Water at Linnels (approximately 20 miles as the crow flies), there is little to recommend it as the site of Arthur's Bassas River battle. Most damaging, there is no stream here.

The other 'tun of Bassa's people' is at the confluence of the Aln and the Shipley and Eglingham Burns not far east of a Roman road that connects Dere Street and the Devil's Causeway. This Bassington is also roughly equidistant between the Northumberland Glen and the Devil's Water/ Dubglas near Hadrian's Wall, and near the Roman fort of Alauna on the Aln at Low Learchild.

Once again, however, there is no stream at Bassington bearing the Bassa name.

In the East Riding of Yorkshire, near Bridlington, there is a place I originally overlooked. This is Bessingby, the by or 'farmstead, village, settlement' of the people of Bassa. The important thing about Bessingby is that there was a Romano- British settlement here (http://www.pastscape.org.uk/hob.aspx?hob_id =1191551) and a Bessingby Beck or stream nearby.

A Roman road ran from Stamford Bridge to Bridlington (http://www.pastscape.org.uk/hob.aspx?hob_id =1029959&sort=4&search=all&criteria=Orby&rational=q&recordsperpage=10) and some believe (see Rivet and Smith) this to be the territory of the Gabrantovices, probably "cavalry fighters" and not "goat fighters". The Gabrantovicum Sinus of Ptolemy would then be Bridlington Bay.

It is quite conceivable that Bessingby Beck was once known simply as "Bassa's Stream".

There is a problem with this placename, however. The –by terminal is Norse, and it is likely, therefore, that the entire name is not from Bassa, but from Bessi. Or, that if Bassa is the name recorded, it would not have become a placename until fairly late. Here is what Alan James had to say on ths subject:

"A. H. Smith's PNERY, 100, which says: 'The first element may be a patronymic formation, "the people of *Basa* or *Besa*", but there is little or no evidence for such -*inga*- formations with OScand **by**. It is therefore more likely to be a patronymic *Basing* or *Besing* with an uninflected genitive. Each name is well recorded... the fo mer may be from OE *Bassa* or OScand *Bassi,* the latter from OScand *Bessi* (a variant of *Bersi....*).

As there is no clear evidence for a change of *a* to *e* in ME, *Besing-* seems more probable, and in that case the less frequent but earlier *Basing-* forms would be Anglo-Norman spelling variants... *Besing's* farmstead'.

Subsequent work, especially by Barrie Cox, has demonstrated that the patronymic '-*inga*-' formations in S and E England (as far north as Yorks) date from the pre-Christian period, so such formations would have been long since obsolete by the time OScand *by* was introduced.

Smith's etymology would imply an Anglo- Scandinavian formation from the late 9th - early 11th ct."

Thus this would seem an unlikely candidate for Arthur's Bassas battle.

The conventional thinking on the Bassas name is to derive the first component from W. bas. Kenneth H. Jackson first discussed this possibility.

According to the Gieriadur Prifysgol Cymru, bas means 'shallow, not deep, fordable; shallows, shallow water'. This would make a great deal of sense for a river-name – or even merely a DESCRIPTION of a river or stretch of a river.

Alan James of BLITON was kind enough to send me the following on bas in place-names:

Bas Late Latin *bassus adopted as Late Brittonic *basso-/ā- > Middle - Modern Welsh bas, Cornish *bas (in compound and place-names, see CPNE p. 18), Breton bas The Latin origin is reasonably certain, though the Late Latin ancestral form seems elusive. 'shallow', adjective. (a2) Bazard Lane Wig (stream-name, New Luce) PNGall p. 34 bas- + -ar, which see [+ SW Scots lane < Gaelic leana, 'a slow, boggy stream']. (c2) Bazil Point Lanc (Overton) PNLanc p. 175 ?bas- + linn, proposed by R. Coates, CVEP p. 318. Oliver Padel Cornish Place-name Elements

Nottingham 1985: *bas 'a shallow', as a noun, 'shallows': only in basdhowr glossing vadum 'a ford' ... the verb occurs, ppp basseys 'abated'... Welsh and Breton bas... [occurs in Cornwall in:] C2) [= specific in name-phrase] Carn Base, coast[al name]; ?Park an Bays f[ie]ld[-name]

Alan James again came to the rescue when I asked how Bassas may have developed out of Late Latin or Late Brittonic:

"By the time the Latin word was adopted by Britt speakers, its inflectional forms were probably quite reduced at least in "vulgar" speech, and the Britt inflextions likewise. So your hypothetical form would be, for practical purposes *bassas. The -as suffix is nominal, noun-forming, it would be 'a shallow, shallows'. I suppose that might be a stream-name, more likely a name for a stretch of a river or a point on a river or estuary, a strategic location where a battle might well be fought, though of course there must be scores of possible candidates."

Long ago the antiquarian Skene suggest Dunipace ner Falkirk in Stirlingshire for Arthur's Bassas. The idea has not been thought well of by scholars over the years. However, recently place-name expert John Reid has tentatively proposed that Dunipace might be rendered Dun y Bas, the 'Hill of the Ford.'

Commenting on this possibility, Alan James shared this with me:

THE ARTHUR OF HISTORY

"It ought to be *din-y-bas, not **dun-y-bais (that's what misled me); it would mean more correctly 'fort of the shallow', which is apparently okay topographically; the changes din > dun, /b/ > /p/, and /a/ > long /a:/ could all be explained in terms of adoption by Gaelic speakers. 'Hills of death' [a local, traditional etymology] would be G *duin-am-bais, which I wouldn't rule out, though I'm uneasy with /mb/ > /p/."

If we may allow for bas here to be for a shallow ford, something rather remarkable occurs: we find ourselves directly between the Dumyat and Myot Hill hillforts which delineate the territory of the ancient Pictish Maeatae. According to the Life of St. Columba by Adomnan, Arthur son of Aedan of Dalriada died fighting the Miathi.

I would then identify the Bassas River with the bas on the Carron. This battle would then be an intrusion into the list of a battle belonging to a later Arthur.

The Irish Annals place the Dalriadan Arthur's death in Circenn. [For Arthur's contest with an opponent at Abernethy on the border of Circenn, see Chapter 4 below.] This has created a major problem, for Circenn is the Pictish province lying to the north of the Firth of Tay and this is quite a distance from the territory of the Miathi. Scholars have tried to account for this confusion over the battle site location in various ways. Bannerman attemtps to offer an explanation (pp. 84-85 Studies in the History of Dalriada) for the two death sites. It would appear several battles had become confused in the Irish annals, with Arthur dying properly in the territory of the Miathi and NOT in Circenn.

However, suppose what we have here is a confused record of battles fought in the North by TWO ARTHURS - one who fought the Miathi at Dunipace/Bassas and another - the Dalriadan one - who was slain while fighting in Circenn?

The Seventh Battle: The Celidon Wood

Caledonia was originally the region of the Great Glen in Highland Scotland inhabited by the Caledonii.

As such, in Classical usage Caledonia came to mean Scotland north of the Forth-Clyde isthmus. But in Welsh tradition - as is evidenced by the presence of Merlin at 1) Arthuret just north of Carlisle, 2) Drumelzier on the Tweed 3) the region near Glasgow, and 4) a mountain in the central Lowlands [see my The Mysteries of Avalon for a discussion of this last) - the Coed Celidon would appear to be at the heart of the Scottish Lowlands. It is generally accepted by scholars that this is indeed the location of the great wood in the Welsh sources.

We may be able to pinpoint the location of the Coed Celidon battle more precisely.

It is possible that a river-name in the area, believed to be a truly ancient hydronym, may have contributed to the idea in early Welsh tradition that Celidon lay in this part of the Scottish Lowlands.

THE ARTHUR OF HISTORY

Caddon Water, a tributary of the Tweed, has a Roman road. The etymology of Caddon (Keleden-lee, 1175, Kaledene, 1296) is interesting.

From Alan James of BLITON:

Nicolaisen included Caddon Water among the *cal-eto- river-names. The final syllable is pro ably OE -denu added by Northumbrian English, though a secondary suffix isn't impossible. It is a very common hydronymic formation; *cal-eddoes indeed occur in ethnic names too ("hard men"), including that of the Calidonii."

When I asked Mr. James whether this name could have contributed to the region thereabouts becoming known as the Celidon Wood, he r sponded:

"Well, yes, a name like *caleden could readily have attracted folk- or learned etymologising and dinnseannachas. I think it would have contracted to something like the modern form Caddon by the 15th ct, so I doubt whether such a thought would have arisen in the early modern period, when renewed interest in Tacitus etc., and even 'Nennius', gave rise to a good deal of fanciful etymologising.

But it's in an area with a good many P-Celtic pns, many of which I consider to be 'late' Cumbric, i.e. 10th-11th ct, when I think there was something of a revival/ reintroduction of the language in the upper Tweed/ Moorfoots/ Lauderdale area, and my hunch is that was the period when Arthurian and other (semi-) legendary associations were being attached to locations in that area, as in the Solway basin.

But I don't think the water-name would have been been given at that time, it's an 'ancient' hydronym that might have come to be associated with Caledonia because of the (accidental) similarity."

There are remnants of a fort at Caddonlee by Caddonfoot (http://canmore.rcahms.gov.uk/en/site/54413/details/caddonlee/). The famous Eildon Hills fort at the Roman period Trimontium on Dere Street is only a dozen or so kilometers to the east of the mouth of the Caddon. Several other hillforts are in the area and a Roman road went from Trimontium west along the Tweed to the Easter Happrew fort beyond Peebles.

The Eighth Battle: Castle Guinnion

The Castle ('Castellum') Guinnion has been identified with the Roman fort of Vinovium at Binchester, although the great Professor Kenneth Jackson thought this unlikely. It has since been noted, however, that Ptolemy's alternative Vinnovium (B. *Uinnouion) brings us very close to the later name set down by Nennius. Vinnovium should have given in Old Welsh at this stage a form in –wy, but it could be that – ion has been maintained as a so-called 'learned form'. Thus the identification should not be rejected.

THE ARTHUR OF HISTORY

Binchester is not far south of Hadrian's Wall on the Roman Dere Street. The fort stands on a spur of high ground some one and a quarter miles north of Bishop Auckland. It overlooks a loop in the river Wear and is in an excellent defensive position.

The fort was built in 79 CE during the Roman advance into northern England. From the early second century Binchester and the other Dere Street forts became important supply depots for Hadrian's Wall and developed as military centres controlling the region south of the Wall.
The fort was in continuous military use until the early years of the 5th century. After the final withdrawal of the garrison the fort and the surrounding vicus (civilian settlement) continued to be occupied by the local, native population and it would seem that Binchester remained an important small town. By the beginning of the 6th century the fort buildings were being torn down and stripped of stone. Part of the site was ut lized by Anglo-Saxons as a cemetery.

I had at one time proposed Carwinning in Dalry parish, Ayrshire, which is from a Caer + Winnian. This looks very good, but if a battle were fought here during Arthur's time it was certainly not against the English.

There are, of course, several "Gwynion" place-names in Wales, but again, none of them work for Arthur.

In passing, I would put forward an additional, though tentative argument in support of Binchester as Guinnion. In the Introduction I alluded to Arthur's carrying of the image of Mary on his shield during the Guinnion battle. It may not be a coincidence that Binchester is known for having a cult of the Mother Goddesses at its Roman fort. It is possible Mary in the Arthurian battle context is a Christian substitution for the Binchester 'Mother.'

From http://theses.univ-lyon2.fr/documents/lyon2/2009/beck_n#p=0&a=top (Goddesses in Roman Religion, thesis by Noemie Beck, 2009):

"In Britain, the dedications to the Matres amount to approximately fifty inscriptions, all but a few from military sites, notably along Antonine's and Hadrian's Wall, and dedicated by soldiers. One of the few exceptions is the inscription to the Matres Ollototae, which is from the non-military site of Heronbridge, Cheshire. This suggests that the cult of the Matres and Matronae was brought to Britain by auxiliary troops from the Continent, such as by the Germanic legionaries of the Roman army. However, it does not mean that the Celtic peoples from Britain did not have any cultural notions of the Mother Goddesses, only that some particularities in the worship must have come with the army. The cult of the Mothers in Britain is clearly Romanized, for they all bear Roman epithets, such as Transmarinae, Campestres, Domesticae or Fatae, apart from the Matres Ollototae and the Matres Suleviae. The Matres Ollototae are undeniably Celtic, for their name is composed of Celtic ollo-, 'all' and teuta, touta, 'tribe'. They are thus 'The Mothers of All the Peoples'. They are mentioned in an inscription from Heronbridge (Claverton, Cheshire): Deabus Matribus Ollototis Iul(ius) Secundus et Aelia Augustina, 'To the Mother Goddesses Ollototae, Julius Secundus and Aelia Augustina (set this up)', and in three inscriptions from Binchester (Durham): Deab(us) Matrib(us) O[l]lot(otis) T[i]b(erius) Cl(audius) Quintianus b(ene)f(iciarius) co(n)s(ularis) v.s.l.m., 'To the Mother Goddesses Ollototae Tiberius Claudius Quintianus beneficiaries of the governor, willingly and deservedly fulfilled his vow' ; [M]atrib(us) O[lloto(tis)] CARTO VAL MARTI Vetto(num) GENIO LOCI LIT . IXT, 'To the Mother Goddesses Ollototae ... Cavalry Regiment of Vettonians....' ; I(ovi) O(ptimo) M(aximo) et Matribus Ollototis sive Transmarinis, 'To Jupiter, Best and Greatest, and to the Ollototae or Overseas Mother Goddesses'."

The Ninth Battle: City of the Legion

The City of the Legion (Urbs Legionis) is, in this context, the Roman legionary fortress at York, the Romano-British Eburacum.

Dere Street began at the fort and ran north to Hadrian's Wall and beyond. The argument against York is that, according to Welsh sources, the only Roman forts called Cities of the Legion were Chester or Deva and Caerleon or Isca. But to claim the Welsh were ignoarant of the fact that York was a legionary fortress seems very doubtful.

To begin, we have chieftains such as Peredur son of Efrauc (Efrauc = Eburacum/'York') and Peredur son of Eliffer (Eleutherius) Gosgordfawr. Peredur is a Welsh rendering of the Roman rank of Praetor. The governor or legate of Britannia Inferior, that is Northern Britain, was in the later period of praetorian rank.

The Roman emperor Caracalla reviewed the administration of Britain and split the province into two: Britannia Superior in the south, which had a consular governor based at London with two legions, the Twentieth at Chester and the Second at Caerleon. Britannia Inferior in the north had a praetorian governor with only one legion, the Sixth at York, where the governor also resided.

The Romans constructed their first fort at Eboracum in 71 CE. The fort's rectangular construction consisted of a V-shaped ditch and earthen ramparts with a timber palisade, interval towers and four gateways. It covered about 50 acres of a grid-plan of streets between timber barrack blocks, storehouses and workshops. More important buildings included the huge Principia (Headquarters Building), the Commandant's House, a hospital and baths. The fort was designed to house the entire legion and remained a military headquarters almost to the end of Roman rule in Britain.

The fortifications at York were strengthened around 80 CE by a caretaker garrison while the Ninth Legion campaigned with the governor, Julius Agricola, in Wales and Scotland. The original fort was replaced in 108 CE by a massive stone structure with walls that survived long enough to be incorporated into the defenses of Viking and even later medieval York.

The one thing that makes York somewhat suspect as an Arthurian battle site is the presence there during the Roman period of the camp prefect Artorius, from whose name Arthur derives. It is certainly possible the memory of this Artorius influenced the placement of the Dark Age Arthur at the fort.

The Tenth Battle: Shore of the River Tribruit

The location of the shore (W. traeth) of the river Tribruit has remained unresolved. The clue to its actual whereabouts may lie in the two possible meanings assigned to this place-name.

According to Kenneth Jackson (_Once Again Arthur's Battles_, MODERN PHILOLOGY, August, 1945), Tribruit, W. tryfrwyd, was used as an adjective, meaning "pierced through", and sometimes as a noun meaning "battle". His rendering of traeth tryfrwyd was "the Strand of the Pierced or Broken (Place)". Basing his statement on the Welsh Traeth Tryfrwyd, Jackson said that "we should not look for a river called Tryfwyd but for a beach." However, Jackson later admitted (in The Arthur of History, ARTHURIAN LITERATURE IN THE MIDDLE AGES: A COLLABORATIVE HISTORY, ed. by Roger Sherman Loomis) that "the name (Traith) Tribruit may mean rather 'The Many-Coloured Strand' (cf. I. Williams in BBCS, xi [1943], 95).

Most recently Patrick Sims-Williams (in The Arthur of the Welsh, THE EARLY WELSH ARTHURIAN POEMS, 1991) has defined traeth tryfrwyd as the "very speckled shore" (try- here being the intensive prefix *tri-, cognate with L. trans). Professor Sims-Williams mentions that 'trywruid' could also mean "bespattered [with blood]." I would only add that Latin litus does usually mean "seashore, beach, coast", but that it can also mean "river bank". Latin ripa, more often used of a river bank, can also have the meaning of "shore".

The complete listing of tryfrwyd from The Dictionary of Wales (information courtesy Andrew Hawke) is as follows:

tryfrwyd
2 [?_try-^2^+brwyd^2^_; dichon fod yma fwy nag un gair [= "poss. more than one word here"]]
3 _a_. a hefyd fel _e?b_.
6 skilful, fine, adorned; ?bloodstained; battle, conflict.
7 12g. GCBM i. 328, G\\6aew yg coryf, yn toryf, yn _tryfrwyd_ - wryaf.
7 id. ii. 121, _Tryfrwyd_ wa\\6d y'm pria\\6d prydir, / Trefred ua\\6r, treul ga\\6r y gelwir.
7 id. 122, Keinuyged am drefred _dryfrwyd_.
7 13g. A 19. 8, ymplymnwyt yn _tryvrwyt_ peleidyr....
7 Digwydd hefyd fel e. afon [="also occurs as river name"] (cf.
8 Hist Brit c. 56, in litore fluminis, quod vocatur _Tribruit_; 14 x CBT
8 C 95. 9-10, Ar traethev _trywruid_).
Tryfrwyd itself, minus the intensive prefix,

comes from:
brwyd
[H. Grn. _bruit_, gl. _varius_, gl. Gwydd. _bre@'t_ `darn']
3 _a_.
6 variegated, pied, chequered, decorated, fine; bloodstained; broken, shattered, frail, fragile.
7 c. 1240 RWM i. 360, lladaud duyw arnam ny am dwyn lleydwyt - _urwyt_ / llauurwyt escwyt ar eescwyd.
7 c. 1400 R 1387. 15-16, Gnawt vot ystwyt _vrwyt_ vriwdoll arnaw.
7 id. 1394. 5-6, rwyt _vrwyt_ vrwydyrglwyf rwyf rwyd get.
7 15g. H 54a. 12.
The editors of GCBM (Gwaith Cynddelw Brydydd) take _tryfrwyd_ to be a fem. noun = 'brwydr'. They refer to Ifor Williams, Canu Aneirin
294, and A.O.H. Jarman, Aneinin: Y Gododdin (in English) p. 194 who translates 'clash', also Jarman, Ymddiddan Myrddin a Thaliesin,
pp. 36-7. Ifor Williams, Bulletin of the Board of Celtic Studies xi (1941-4) pp. 94-6 suggests
try+brwyd `variegated, decorated'.
On brwydr, the National Dictionary of Wales has this:
1 brwydr^1^
2 [dichon ei fod o'r un tarddiad a@^ _brwyd^1^_, ond cf. H. Wydd. _bri@'athar_ `gair']
3 _eb_. ll. -_au_.
6 pitched battle, conflict, attack, campaign, struggle; bother, dispute, controversy; host, army.

7 13g. HGC 116, y lle a elwir . . . y tir gwaetlyt, o achaus y _vrwyder_ a vu ena.
7 14g. T 39. 24.
7 14g. WML 126, yn dyd kat a _brwydyr_.
7 14g. WM 166. 32, _brwydreu_ ac ymladeu.
7 14g. YCM 33, llunyaethu _brwydyr_ a oruc Chyarlymaen, yn eu herbyn.
7 15g. IGE 272, Yr ail gofal, dial dwys, / _Brwydr_ Addaf o Baradwys.
7 id. 295.
7 1567 LlGG (Sall) 14a, a' chyd codei _brwydyr_ im erbyn, yn hyn yr ymddiriedaf.
7 1621 E. Prys: Ps 32a, Yno drylliodd y bwa a'r saeth, / a'r _frwydr_ a wnaeth yn ddarnau.
7 1716 T. Evans: DPO 35, Cans _brwydr_ y Rhufeiniaid a aethai i Si@^r Fo@^n.
7 1740 id. 336, _Brwydrau_ lawer o Filwyr arfog.

Dr. G. R. Isaac of The University of Wales, Abe ystywyth, in discussing brwyd, adds that:

"The correct Latin comparison is frio 'break up', both < Indo-European *bhreiH- 'cut, graze'. These words have many cognates, e.g. Latin fr uolus 'friable, worthless', Sanskrit bhrinanti 'they damage', Old Church Slavonic britva 'razor', and others. The Old British form of brwyd would have been *breitos. It is sometimes claimed that there is a possible Gaulish root cognate in brisare 'press out', but there are difficulties with that identification.

It may be worth stressing that the 'tryfrwyd' which means 'very speckled' and the 'tryfrwyd' which means 'piercing, pierced' are the same word, and that the latter is the historically pri mary meaning. The meaning 'very speckled' comes through 'bloodstained' from 'pierced' ('bloodstained' because 'pierced' in battle). But I do not think this has any bearing on the arguments.

Actually, Tryfrwyd MAY mean 'very speckled', but that is conjecture, not certain knowledge. Plausible conjecture, yes, but no more certain for that."

That "pierced" or "broken" is to be preferred as the meaning of Tribruit is plainly demonstrated by lines 21-22 of the _Pa Gur_ poem:

Neus tuc manauid - "Manawyd(an) brought
Eis tull o trywruid - pierced ribs (or, metaphorically, "timbers", and hence arms of any kind, probably spears or shields;) from Tryfrwyd"

Tull, "pierced", here obviously refers to Tribruit as "through-pierced".

Professor Hywel Wyn Owen, Director of the Place-Name Research Centre, University of Wales Bangor, has the following to say on traeth + river names (personal correspondence):

"There are only two examples of traeth + river name that I know of, both in Anglesey (Traeth Dulas, Traeth Llugwy) but there may well be others. The issue is still the same however. Where a river flows into the sea would normally be aber. The traeth would only be combined with the river name if the river name was also used of a wider geographical context, and became, say, the name of the bay. Hence traeth + bay name rather than traeth + river name directly."

In the poem, the shore of Tryfrwyd battle is listed one just prior to Din Eidyn and once just after the same fort (I will have more on the Pa Gur battle sites below). The Gwrgi Garwllwyd or 'Man-dog Rough-grey' who is also placed at Tryfrwyd has been associated with the Cynbyn or 'Dog-heads' Arthur fought at Din Eidyn.

Manawyd's role at Tryfrwyd may suggest that this river or its shore is to be found in or on the borders of Manau Gododdin, which was the district round the head of the Firth of Forth, whose name remains in Slamannan and Clackmannan.

The Fords of Frew west of Stirling have been proposed as the site of the battle, but Jackson claims W. frut or ffrwd, 'stream', cannot have yielded frwyd. Jackson also countered Skene's theory that this was the Forth, on the grounds that the Welsh name for the Forth, Gweryd, which would be *Guerit in OW.

The poem may be even more specific, in that Traeth Tryfrwyd is said to be 'ar eidin cyminauc' (line 28), 'at Eidyn on the border'. Now, the 'bo der' here could be the Firth of Forth, but it is much more likely to be the line of division between Gododdin proper and Manau Gododdin.

The Cynbyn or 'Dog-heads' may partly owe their existence to the Coincenn daughter of Aedan, father of the Dalriadan Arthur, and to the Coinchend in the Irish story The Adventure of Art son of Conn. In this Irish tale, Art battles a monstrous woman named Coincenn or 'Doghead' who is a member of a tribe bearing the same name."

The name of Art son of Conn's mother may be significant in this context. She was called Eithne, which was also the name of the mother of the god Lugh. The place-name Eidyn is of u known etymology. Because Din Eidyn was the capital of Lothian, and Lothian is derived from Middle Welsh Lleudinyawn, Brittonic *Lugudunia:non, land of 'Lugh's (W. Lleu's) Fo tress', it would be reasonable to suggest that Eidyn as Lugh's fortress represents a British form of Irish Eithne. Din Eidyn would then be the Fort of (the goddess) Eithne.

The Coincenn of the Irish are thought to be a reflection of the Classical Cynacephali.

Ole Munch-Pedersen cites the following note from Cecile Ó Rahilly text of the Irish heroic epic Cath Finntrágha or the "Battle of the White Strand" (Irish traigh is cognate with Welsh traeth):

"The Coinchinn or Coinchennaig are frequently mentioned in Irish literature. From the 8th century on the name was applied to pirates who ravaged Ireland. Cp. Thurneysen, Zu Ir. Hss., p. 24. In the Adventures of Art mac Cuinn they are represented as living in Tir na nIngnad whose King is called Conchruth (Éiriu III. 168). They are mentioned in a poem in the Book of the Dean of Lismore (Rel. Celt. I. 80) and in a poem is Duanaire Finn (xxxviii) where they are said to have invaded Ireland and been defeated by Finn. In the YBL tale Echtra Clérech Choluim Cille (RC XXVI 160 § 45, 161 § 48) men with dogs' heads are 'of the race of Ham or of Cain'. Similarly in the late romance Síogra Dubh the Caitcheannaigh and Coincheannaigh and Gabharcheannaigh are said to be do chinéal Caim mic Naoi (GJ XIX 99 5-6, cp. LU 122)." (Cath Finntrágha, (1962), lch. 65).

From the English translation of the Battle of Ventry/Cath Finntragha (http://www.maryjones.us/ctexts/f20.html):

"'O soul, O Glas son of Dreman,' said the king of the world, 'not a harbour like this didst thou promise my fleet would find, but shores of white sand where my army might assemble for fairs and gatherings whenever they were not fighting.' 'I know a harbour like that in the west of Erinn,' said Glas, 'namely, Ventry Harbour... They went onward thence to Ventry, and filled the borders of the whole harbour so that the sea was not visible between them, and the great barque of the king of the world was the first to take harbour, so that thenceforward its name was Rinn na Bairci (The Point of the Barque). And they let down their many-coloured linen-white sails, and raised their purple-mouthed speckled tents, and consumed their excellent savoury viands, and their fine intoxicating drinks, and their harps were brought to them for long playing, and their poets to sing their songs and their dark conceits to them...

THE ARTHUR OF HISTORY

Now, these hosts and armies came into Ciarraige Luachra and to red-maned Slieve Mis, and thence to Ventry Harbour. 'O Tuatha De Danand,' said Abartach, 'let a high spirit and courage arise within you in the face of the battle of Ventry. For it will last for a day and a year, and the deed of every single man of you will be related to the end of the world, and fulfil now the big words ye have uttered in the drinking- houses.' 'Arise,O Glas, son of Dreman,' said Bodb Derg the son of the Dagda ,'to announce combat for me to the king of the world.' Glas went where the king of the world was. 'O soul, O Glas,' said the king of the world, 'are those yonder the fianns of Erinn?' 'Not they,' said Glas, 'but another lot of the men of Erinn, that dare not to be on the surface of the earth, but live in sid-brugs (fairy mansions) under the ground, called the Tuatha De Danand, and to announce battle from them have I come.' 'Who will answer the Tuatha De Danand for me?' said the king of the world. 'We will go against them,' said two of the kings of the world, namely, Comur Cromgenn, the king of the men of the Dogheads, and Caitch-enn, the king of the men of the Catheads, and they had five red-armed battalions in order, and they went on shore forthwith in their great red waves.

'Who is there to match the king of the men of the Dogheads for me?' said Bodb Derg. 'I will go against him,'said Lir of Sid Finnachaid,'though I have heard that there is not in the great world a man of stronger arm than he.'"

It is the Dogheads who would appear to hold the key to unravelling the Traeth Tryfrwyd mystery.

Thanks to Lothian native and place-name expert John Wilkinson, who consulted a friend on the matter, I have learned the following:

"Ardchinnechena<n> is a place which the St. Andrews Foundation Account B says was where Hungus son of Forso placed the head of the defeated Saxon king Athelstan on a pole "within the harbour which is now called Queen's Ferry" (i.e. North Queensferry?); and which the shorter Account calls Ardchinnechun. Simon Taylor's Fife Vol 3 offers 'height/promontory of the head' for the first and hints at a dindshenchas containing con 'dog' (in genitive) for the second."

Ardchinnechena[n] is generally supposed to be the headland used by the Railway Bridge (see "Place-names of Fife", vol. 1, 381-2, vol.3, 582-3).

This 'Height of the Dog's Head' in North Queensferry Harbor reinforces my view that the Welsh tryfrwyd, 'through-piered', is an attempt to translate Latin trajectus, which has the exact literal meaning. However, trajectus also was the word used for a river-crossing, like the one at Queensferry.

The Eleventh Battle: Mount Agned and/or Mount Breguoin

Mount Breguoin, found only in late rescensions of the Historia Brittonum has been associated with the 'cellawr Brewyn' or cells of Brewyn where Urien of Rheged later fought, a site generally agreed to be the Roman fort of Bremenium at High Rochester on Dere Street. Kenneth Jackson, who thought the name might also be an interpolation, came to this conclusion ("Arthur's Battle of Breguoin", ANTIQUITY 23, Jan 1 1949, p. 48). Most scholars now think that the Breguoin battle was taken from the Urien poem and incorporated into the Arthurian battle-list in the HB. As Arthur was linked to the Welsh word arth, 'bear', it may not be a coincidence that a bear god named Matunus was worshipped at Bremenium during the Roman period.

Mount Agned has hitherto escaped philological analysis. From Kenneth Jackson's time on, one original form proposed has been Angned. But this is an unknown word and has failed to produce a viable site. Most authorities feel that Agned is a corruption.

The simplest explanation for Agned as a corrupt form has been supplied by Dr. Andrew Breeze of the University of Navarre. Dr. Breeze proposed that the /n/ of Agned should be read as a /u/. This is a brilliant solution to the problem, although his attempt to then identify Agned with Pennango or Penangushope near Hawick is seriously flawed. I would see in this last a Pen, "headland", plus the Gaelic personal name Angus. As Alan James makes clear,

"We know in that area in the heart of the Southern Uplands, P-, Q-Celtic, Anglian and Scandinavian pers names were being used promiscuously, irrespective of the language or ethnicity of the bearers, and P-Celtic was probably still current late enough for a pen- to be named after an Angus."

Penangushope would be 'the narrow/enclosed valley of Angus's Headland.'

Dr. Graham Isaac has the following to say on the idea that Agned could represent an original Agued:

"The n > u copying error is a common one. The word agued is a rare one, and is used only three times in the early materials. It means something like 'dire straits, difficulty, anxiety'."

The most important use of this word, for the present purpose, is found in Canu Aneirin line 1259, where it occurs in the phrase 'twryf en agwed', 'a host in dire straits'. We will return to this phrase in a moment.

We have discussed the possibility that the Arthur section in HB represents a Latin retelling of an OW heroic poem. Such a poem could have had a line in it like 'galon in agued', 'the enemy in dire straits, great difficulty', much like the Canu Aneirin's 'twryf en agwed'. It is conceivable that an author responsible for the Harleian recension of the HB (who may not have been entirely versed in the diction of OW heroic poetry) may have mistaken this 'agued' for a actual place-name, and wrongly placed the battle there: instead of 'the enemy in dire straits', he understood 'the enemy at Agued', easily miscopied.

Under this interpretation, the only location for the battle that was ever correct was Breguoin/Bremenium. This analysis at least solves the problem of 'Where was Agned?' with the answer, 'There never was such a place, and so no need to look for it.'

What we may have in 'Mount Agued', then, is a confused reference to a battle at Mount Breguoin/Bremenium where the enemy found itself 'in dire straits'. If so, we would have four, and possibly five battles said to have been fought by Arthur on Dere Street: York, Binchester, Devil's Water, Celidon Wood and High Rochester.

The argument against Bremenium/High Rochester as an Arthurian battle, which relies upon the presence of gellawr brewyn, the 'cells of Brem nium', in the Urien battle poem list, ignores the very real possibility that more than one battle could have been fought at Bremenium at different times. Bremenium is situated in a very strategic position, essentially guarding the pass over which Dere Street crosses the Cheviots. It is also true that Urien's Brewyn could just as easily have been borrowed from the Arthurian battle-list as the other way around.

While it may well be that Agued/Agned is merely an error for Bregouin or a poetic name for the latter, there is a second possible identification for this Arthurian battle site. The 'Twryf yn aguedd' phrase mentioned above comes from the 'Gwarchan Tudfwlch', a poem appended to The Gododdin.

What is surprising about the 'Gwarchan Tu fwlch' example is that the phrase is preceded by two lines that copy part of a line found in Strophe 25 of The Gododdin proper:

"Arf anghynnull, Anghyman ddull, Twryf en agwed..."
"Arf anghynnull, anghyman ddull..."

Now, in the case of The Gododdin line, the poet Aneirin is referring to Graid son of Hoywgi's prowess at the disastrous battle of Catraeth, Roman Cataractonium, modern-day Catterick on Dere Street in Yorkshire. The Battle of Catraeth is, of course, the subject of The Gododdin poem.

The hero Tudfwlch hailed from the region of Eifionydd in Gwynedd, but he fought and died at Catraeth. While he engaged in military actions in his homeland (the 'Gwarchan's' 'Dal Henban' is almost certainly modern Talhenbont at Llanystumdwy in Eifionydd), it is probable that the lines borrowed from The Gododdin are meant to indicate that the following 'Twryf yn aguedd', 'a host in distress', is a reference to the British army at Catraeth.

Dr. Graham agrees with me on this assessment, saying that

"Phrases like twryf yn aguedd are characteristically used in early Welsh poetry to set up a general atmosphere of warrior violence, but, to judge from the final lines of the poem, it would seem to be primarily concerned with the 'Battle of Catraeth'."

Part of the Roman fort at Catterick was built on the rising ground above the River Swale known as Thornbrough Hill. And Arthur is mentioned in Line 972 of The Gododdin. Whether this is an interpolation or not, it is generally thought to be one of the earliest occurrences of his name in the written records:

"He fed black ravens on the rampart of a fortress
Though he was no Arthur.
Among the powerful ones in battle,
In the front rank, Gwawrddur was a palisade."

Are we to see as a coincidence Arthur's being mentioned in the context of the Battle of Catraeth when it is in this same battle, alone among all battles of the period, that a host finds itself in 'agued'?

There are two possible ways to read this passage on Arthur in The Gododdin. First, the hero Gwawrddur, while a great warrior, was not nearly as great as Arthur. This is the standard interpretation. But let us suppose that what is really meant is that Arthur had fought at Catterick as well, a generation earlier, only he proved more powerful than Gwawrddur and won a victory over the Saxons on Thornbrough Hill, i.e. Mount Agned.

In this context, the Arthurian Mount Agned of the HB could be an anachronistic reference to the hill at Cataractonium, where the British army of Gwawrddur's time found itself in 'distress' or 'dire straits' just prior to its annihilation by the Saxon foe.

So if we assume Agned = Agued = Catterick, where did Arthur fight – at High Rochester or Catraeth?

Well, the simple answer is 'Either, both or neither.' If Breguoin is indeed borrowed from the Urien poem, then Arthur did not fight at High Rochester. If Agned is Thornborough Hill at Catterick, then the site may have been chosen merely because his name was mentioned in The Gododdin.

Almost the entire defensive circuit of the High Rochester/Bremenium fort is preserved, with the remains of the western gateway being particularly fine. There is also evidence of several periods of rebuilding in the western intervaltower of the south side. The ditches are well preserved to the north and east, outside which the line of Dere Street marches north-west. Between the thick stone ramparts the fort measures around 440 ft north-south by about 420 ft east-west, giving an occupation area of about 4.25 acres. There are inner stone buildings.

On the north, the remains of as many as thirteen ditches can be distinguished. On the east and south, four, and six ditches curve around the north-west angle. It is unknown how many ditches were on the west side of the fort.

The Roman fort at Catterick was likely founded during the early 70 CE's to guard the crossing of Dere Street over the River Swale. At the very latest, the fort must have been in place by 79 CE, in order to guard the northern supply route of Agricola's Scottish campaigns. After an undetermined period of neglect, it would appear that the fort was recommissioned during the administration of Gnaeus Julius Verus in the aftermath of the Brigantian revolt of 155 CE, at which time the Antonine Wall was abandoned and the troops pulled back to Hadrian's Wall in order to control the Brigantes. No trace of the fort remains, as it was overlain by the town of Catterick. A crop-mark east of Catterick Rac course has been identified as a Roman temporary camp not far from the fort.

Geoffrey of Monmouth and Agned/Breguoin

Geoffrey of Monmouth's treatment of the Agned name has led to further confusion – although at least in one sense he made have been on the righ track.

To begin, he calls Agned both Maiden Castle and the Dolorous Mountain. While there are many Maiden Castles in Britain, because Edinburgh came to be called this in the medieval period it has been customary to identify the latter with Agned. Geoffrey's thinking here may be identical with that of later antiquarian writers who saw in Agned the Latin Agnetis for St. Agnes, the virgin martyr-saint.

Dr. Simon Rodway of the University of Wales agrees that Agned as found in the HB could have quite regularly and perfectly developed from Agnetis.

The Dolorous Mountain of Geoffrey may well represent his attempt to render Breguoin. Welsh has the following words (GPC listing) which have meanings similar to Latin dolorosus (dolor, doleo):

"gwŷn

[?o'r gwr. *u̯en-, u̯enə- 'ymegnïo am; chwennych, caru, ymfodloni; ymdrechu, llafurio' fel yn y Llad. venus, -eris]

eg.b. ll. gwyniau, gwniau.

Poen, gofid, dolur, brath, artaith; nwyd, angerdd, anian, mympwy; sêl, serch; chwant, drygchwant, anlladrwydd; eiddigedd, dicter, digofaint, llid, cynddaredd:

pain, trouble, ache, smart, pang; passion, emotion, humour, whim; zeal, affection; desire, lust, wantonness; jealousy, displeasure, wrath, rage, fury.

cwyn

[Gwydd. cóine 'wylofain']

eb.g. ll. cwynion, cwynau.

a Achwyniad, datganiad o anghyfiawnder neu o gam, o ofid neu o alar, achos anghydfod neu ofid; galar, gofid:

complaint, plaint, grievance, lament, cause of contention or grief; grief."

An imagined Bre, 'hill', plus this gwyn or cwyn would give a Hill of Pain or Lamentation Mountain. If I'm right about this, then Geoffrey had before him one of the MSS. of the HB which listed both Breguoin and Agned. As the MSS. can identify the two places, Geoffrey followed suit. Thus Agned became Maiden Castle and Breguoin became the Dolorous Mountain.

None of this helps us with the location of Agned, however – if we accept the name as a W. form of L. Agnetis. The few St. Agnes place-names in Britain are all of recent origin. One such exampl is a farm in Scottish Borders, at the confluence of the Whiteadder and Bothwell rivers, near Cranshaws, called St. Agnes. Only a quarter mile of so from this St. Agnes there is a hillfort. What follows is from the CANMORE database:

"NT 682 632 Fort, St Agnes (Stenton). A curvilinear fort with double ramparts and ditches on the end of the spur that lies between the Whiteadder Water and the Bothwell Water, a quarter of a mile WNW of St Agnes. At some former time the Whiteadder has washed into the base of the spur at this point, and the ensuing landslips have destroyed the whole of the south side of the fort. It seems probable, however, that the work was oval on plan and measured internally 300ft from E to

W by some 250ft from N to S. The ramparts which are still visible (just) on the ground at the W end of the fort, are 50ft apart measured from crest to crest, but their original widths can only be determined by excavation."

David N. Haire, an expert in East Lothian history, kindly forward the following information to me concerning St. Agnes in Scottish Borders:

"The first appearance that I have found is St Agnus (not Agnes) on William Forrest's 'Map of Haddingtonshire' 1799/1802. This map associates the place with Sir James Sootie Bart. It is St Agnes on John Ainslie's 'Map of the Southern Part of Scotland' 1821 and on the first Ordnance Survey 6 inches to one mile map. This baronet (usually spelled Suttie) was apparently an undistinguished and reactionary parliamentarian, described as 4th baronet of Balgone and Agnes (without the St).

http://www.historyofparliamentonline.org/volume/1820-1832/member/grant-suttie-sir-james-1759-1836 .

Earlier baronets apparently had only the title 'of Balgone'

http://www.thepeerage.com/p42528.htm .

Given that St Agnes is in a very sharp point between the Bothwell and Whiteadder Waters, my extremely tentative guess was that the name was originally a minor topographical name, possibly Scots aik-ness, meaning 'oak promontory'; and that the ambitious but apparently rather dim baronet tried to add to his status by glorifying his patch of hill land with the prefix St which happened to fit the name. However, the probability of a wholly whimsical name is raised by this family tree which shows that the fourth baronet's mother was Agnes née Grant.

http://www.prestoungrange.org/prestoungrange/archive/history/the-barony-of-prestongrange.pdf"

Agned from Agnetis would, in this context, reside only in Geoffrey's imagination.

Does it make sense, though, to conclude that Mount Agned is a mistake for the agued/agwed of the Gododdin poem? Alas, attractive though this solution is, it does not seem very likely. If one had access to the Gododdin, why not simply say Arthur fought at Catraeth?

Well, as it happens there another very exciting candidate for Agned available to us. A Roman inscription was found at Bremenium/High Rochester with the word EGNAT clearly carved upon it. The full reading of this stone is as follows (from http://romaninscriptionsofbritain.org/inscriptions/1262):

"To the Genius of our Lord and of the standards of the First Cohort of Vardulli and of the Unit of Scouts of Bremenium, styled Gordianus, Egnatius Lucilianus, emperor's propraetorian legate, (set this up) under the charge of Cassius Sabinianus, tribune."

This Egnatius was the governor of Britannia Inferior, i.e. Northern Britain, and as such would have been based at York. He is known from another stone as well, found at Lanchester (http://romaninscriptionsofbritain.org/inscriptions/1091):

"The Emperor Caesar Marcus Antonius Gordianus Pius Felix Augustus erected from ground-level this bath-building with basilica through the agency of Egnatius Lucilianus, emperor's propraetorian legate, under the charge of Marcus Aurelius Quirinus, prefect of the First Cohort of Lingonians, styled Gordiana."

There has been some speculation concerning this man, who may have been of very famous stock (see Inge Mennen's "Power and Status in the Roman Empire, AD 193-284, note 79, p. 101). In any case, as a governor and a rebuilder of forts, his name may have been become attached to that of Bremenium in a sort of nickname fashion – 'the hill of Egnatius' or, as it came down to us in the HB, Mount Agned. Such a nickname may have been purely a local or even legendary development. A good comparison to Bremenium as Egnatius's hill would the Uxellodunum fort at Stanwix, called Petriana after its military garrison.

According to Dr. Simon Roday of the University of Wales,

"Agned cannot derive regularly from Egnatius, but I don't think it's impossible - as you say, there are examples of a- ~ e- in Welsh (agwyddor ~ egwyddor etc). Perhaps a sort of metathesis?"

The examples I had cited were merely a handful I had culled from some of the early Welsh poems:

engai, angai, engis, angwy, etc.

edewi, adaw, adawai, edewid

endewid, andaw

ail, eil

Doubtless more such instances of /a/ for /e/ could be found in other texts.

In answer to the criticism that the Egn- of Egnatius would have undergone a sound change to Ein- by the 9th century, Dr. Rodway added: "Old Welsh spelling was conservative in this respect, so it would be quite regular for the g to still be written."

If I'm right about this, then the Breguoin and Agned place-names both designate the same site – the Bremenium Roman fort at High Rochester.

The Twelfth Battle: Mount Badon

Badon is a difficult place-name for an unexpected reason. As Kenneth Jackson proclaimed:

"No such British name is known, nor any such stem." [To be briefly mentioned in the context of Badon is the Middle Welsh word bad, 'plague, pestilence, death' (GPC; first attested in the 14th century), from Proto-Celtic *bato-, cf. Old Irish bath. Some have asked me whether this word could be the root of Badon - to which Dr. Graham I. Isaac, of the National University of Ireland, Galway, responds emphatically, "No, absolutely no. A (modern) W form _bad_ etc. would have been spelt in the W of the ancient period as _bat_ and there can be no connection since _Bad(on)_ is what we find." Other noteworthy Celtic linguists, such as Dr. Simon Rodway of Aberystwyth University, Dr. Richard Coates of the University of the West of England and Professor Ranko Matasovic of the University of Zagreb, agree with Isaac on this point. Matasovic adds: "Professor Isaac is right; since we have references to Badon in Early Welsh sources, the name would have been spelled with –t- (for voiced /d/). The spelling where the letter <d> stands for /d/ and <dd> for the voiced dental fricative was introduced in the late Middle Ages."]

Graham Isaac has the following to say on the nature of the word Badon, which I take to be authoritative.

His explanation of why Gildas's Badon cannot be derived from one of the Badburys (like Liddington Castle, often cited as a prime candidates for

Badon) is critical in an eventual identification of this battle site. Although long and rather complicated, his argument is convincing and I have, therefore, opted to present it unedited:

"Remember in all that follows that both the -d - in Badon and the -th- in OE Bathum are pronounced like th in 'bathe' and Modern Welsh -dd-. Remember also that in Old English spelling, the letters thorn and the crossed d are interchangeable in many positions: that is variation in spelling, not in sound, and has no significance for linguistic arguments.

It is curious that a number of commentators have been happy to posit a 'British' or 'Celtic' form Badon. The reason seems to be summed up succinctly by Tolstoy in the 1961 article (p. 145):

'It is obviously impossible that Gildas should have given a Saxon name for a British locality'.

Why? I see no reason at all in the world why he should not do so (begging the question as to what, exactly, is the meaning of 'British locality' here; Gildas is just talking about a hill). This then becomes the chief crutch of the argument, as shown on p. 147 of Tolstoy's article: 'But that there was a Celtic name 'Badon' we know from the very passage in Gildas under discussion'.

But that is just circular: ' "Badon" must be "Celic" because Gildas only uses "Celtic" names'. This is no argument. What would have to be shown is that 'Badon' is a regular reflex of a securely attested 'Celtic' word. This is a matter of empirical detail and is easily tested; we have vast resources to tell us what was and was not a 'Celtic' word. And there is nothing like 'Badon'.

So what do we do? Do we just say that 'Badon' must be Celtic because Gildas uses it? That gets us nowhere.

So what of the relationships between aet Bathum - Badon - Baddanbyrig? The crucial point is just that OE Bathum and the Late British / very early Welsh Badon we are talking about both have the soft -th- sound of 'bathe' and Mod.Welsh 'Baddon'. Baddanbyrig, however, has a long d-sound like -d d- in 'bad day'. Both languages, early OE and Late British, had both the d-sound and the soft th-sound. So:

1) If the English had taken over British (hypothetical and actually non-existent) *Badon (*Din Badon or something), they would have made it *Bathanbyrig or the like, and the modern names of these places would be something like *Bathbury.

2) If the British had taken over OE Baddanbyrig, they would have kept the d-sound, and Gildas would have written 'Batonicus mons', and Annales Cambriae would have 'bellum Batonis', etc. (where the -t- is the regular early SPELLING of the sound -d-; always keep your conceptions of spellings and your conceptions of sounds separate; one of the classic errors of the untrained is to fail to distinguish these).

I imagine if that were the case we would have no hesitation is identifying 'Baton' with a Badbury place. But the d-sound and the soft th -sound are not interchangeable. It is either the one or the other, and in fact it is the soft th -sound that is in 'Badon', and that makes it equivalent to Bathum, not Baddanbyrig.

(That applies to the sounds. On the other hand there is nothing strange about the British making Bad-ON out of OE Bath -UM. There was nothing in the Late British/early Welsh language which corresponded to the dative plural ending -UM of OE, so it was natural for the Britons to substitute the common British suffix - ON for the very un-British OE suffix -UM: this is not a substitution of SOUNDS, but of ENDINGS, which is quite a different matter. That Gildas then makes an unproblematic Latin adjective with -icus out of this does not require comment.)

To conclude:

1) There is no reason in the world why a 6thcentury British author should not refer to a place in Britain by its OE name.
2) There was no 'British' or 'Celtic' *Badon.
3) 'Badon' does not correspond linguistically with OE Baddanbyrig.
4) 'Badon' is the predictably regular Late British / early Welsh borrowing of OE Bathum.

Final note: the fact that later OE sources occasionally call Bath 'Badon' is just a symptom of the book-learning of the authors using the form.

Gildas was a widely read and highly respected author, and Badon(-is) (from Gildas's adjective Badon -icus) will quickly and unproblematically have become the standard book-form (i.e. primarily Latin form) for the name of Bath. Again, all attempts to gain some sort of linguistic mileage from the apparent, but illusory, OE variation between Bathum and Badon are vacuous."

It is thus safe to say that 'Badon' must derive from a Bath name. However, we must not restrict ourselves to the Southern Bath, which makes no sense in the context of a Northern Arthur.

For as it happens, there is a major Northern 'Bath' site that has gone completely unnoticed!

In the the High Peak District of Derbyshire we find Buxton. This town had once been roughly on the southernmost boundary of Brigantian tribal territory (thought to lie along a line roughly from the Mersey in the west to the Humber in the east). It was also just within Britannia Inferior (that part of northern Britain ruled from York), whose boundary was again from the Mersey, but probably more towards The Wash.

In the Roman period, Buxton was the site of Aquae Arnemetiae, 'the waters in front of (the goddess) Nemetia'. To the best of our knowledge, Bath in Somerset and Buxton in Derbyshire were the only two 'Aquae' towns in Britain.

But even better, there is a Bathum name extant at Buxton. The Roman road which leads to Buxton from the northeast, through the Peak hills, is called Bathamgate. Batham is 'baths', the exact dative plural we need to match the name Bathum/Badon. -gate is 'road, street', which comes from ME gate, itself a derivative of OScand gata. Bathamgate is thus 'Baths Road'.

The recorded forms for Bathamgate are as follows:

Bathinegate (for Bathmegate), 1400, from W. Dugdale's Monasticon Anghcanum, 6 vols, London
1817-1830.
Bathom gate, 1538, from Ancient Deeds in the Public Record Office
Batham Gate, 1599, from records of the Duchy of Lancaster Special Commissions in the Public Record Office.

Buxton sits in a bowl about one thousand feet above sea level surrounded by mountains and is itself a mountain spa. The natural mineral water of Buxton emerges from a group of springs at a constant temperature of 82 degrees Fahrenheit and is, thus, a thermal water. There are also cold springs and a supply of chalybeate (iron bearing) water. The evidence of Mesolithic man suggests a settlement dating to about 5000 BCE and archaeological finds in the Peak District around the settlement show habitation through the Neolithic, Bronze and Iron Ages to the time of the Romans.

From the historical evidence we can say that Buxton was a civilian settlement of some importance, situated on the intersection of several roads, and providing bathing facilities in warm mineral waters. In short, it was a Roman spa. Place-names in and around Buxton, and Anglo-Saxon finds in burial mound excavations, suggest a continuing inhabitation of the area and probable use of the mineral waters.

It has long been speculated that we should expect to find a military installation at Buxton. However, subsequent archaeological fieldwork, including excavations, in and around suggested locations at the spa town have singularly failed to establish a military presence. A 'ditch feature' identified initially through resistivity survey and then from aerial photography above Mill Cliff, Buxton, gave rise to the almost confident interpretation of this site as being that of the fort: subsequent evaluation in advance of development, however, has shown that these features were geological rather than man-made, and the absence of Roman finds of any description from a series of evaluation trenches suggests that if Buxton had a fort it was located elsewhere.

Today, the site of the probable Roman baths is covered by the Georgian Crescent building. In this area during the seventeenth and eighteenth century discoveries of lead lined baths, red plaster and building remains were made at some considerable depth in the sediments which surround the area of St Anne's well. In the eighteenth century, Pilkington investigated a mound overlooking the site of the previous discoveries. Here he found a structure which has been interpreted as a probable classical temple -

one of only three known from Britain. In the mid-seventies, following the removal of a 20th century swimming pool, a brick structure was exposed and a deposit containing 232 Roman coins, 3 bronze bracelets and a wire clasp ranging in date from the 1st to the end of the 4th century CE was excavated.

This intriguing series of early discoveries lends tangible support to the interpretation of Buxton as the 'Bath of the North', but the character and extent of civilian settlement - and whether this was in association with a military installation or not, remains obscure. A considerable range of small finds, together with occasional glimpses of apparently Roman contexts, from the backgardens of houses has failed to provide a clear sense of the extent of Roman Buxton, let alone a soundly based understanding of its chronology and development. The dating of coinage in the 'votive' deposit from near the Crescent might be seen to indicate heightened frequencies of offerings during the third and fourth centuries. To what extent this might correlate with the development of settlement at Buxton is a matter of some conjecture.

At Poole's cavern, Buxton, excavations between 1981 and 1983 by Peakland Archaeological Society and Buxton Archaeological Society produced a large Romano-British assemblage containing a considerable body of metalwork including coins and brooches, rolls of thin sheet bronze, along with ceramics, a faunal assemblage and burials. The dating of the coins and fibulae point to use between the late 1st and 3rd centuries, with the majority being of 2nd century date. Indeed, reanalysis of the material has suggested that the cave saw its principal period of use between 120 and 220 CE. The excavators appeared to reveal some spatial separation of the coin and fibulae finds from the pottery and faunal remains, although this has been questioned. Discussing the possible character of the use of the site Bramwell and Dalton draw attention to the comparative absence of spindle whorls, loom weights and bone hairpins which might be expected from a domestic site. Instead, they see the evidence as supporting the interpretation of the site as that of a rural shrine or sanctuary.

This too has subsequently been questioned and rejected. Instead, Branigan and Dawley interpret the site as essentially domestic, but with the additional refuse from a metalworker's activities. They see a link between Poole's Cavern and the growth of Buxton as a spa centre providing a ready local market for small decorative trinkets.

The general trend of the evidence suggests that the Roman site may have consisted of a temple overlooking a set of Roman baths. At Bath we have a clear idea of the layout of a significant bath/water shrine complex which consisted of two major ranges: a temple and a religious precinct, within which lay the sacred spring; alongside this range were a line of three baths within a major building, at one end of which lay a typical Roman bathhouse or sauna. The Bath buildings were lavishly built in a classical style and the whole complex attracted visitors from outside the province.

THE ARTHUR OF HISTORY

In essence the Buxton layout mirrors that a Bath: parallel to the spring line is a temple and alongside the springs is a range of possibly Roman baths. As the Buxton temple is two-thirds the size of that at Bath we could assume the Buxton complex was somewhat smaller.

If the grove of the goddess Nemetia continued as an important shrine well into Arthur's time (and the presence of St. Anne's Well at the site of the town's ancient baths shows that the efficacy of the sacred waters was appropriated by Christians), there is the possibility the Saxons targeted Buxton for exactly this reason. Taking the Britons' shrine would have struck them a demoralizing blow. If the goddess or saint or goddess-become-saint is herself not safe from the depredations of the barbarians, who is?

A threat to such a shrine may well have galvanized British resistence. Arthur himself may have been called upon to lead the British in the defense of Nemetia's waters and her temple-grove.

There may be a very good reason why Gildas (or his source, or a later interpolator) may have opted for English Bathum (rendered Badon in the British language of the day). The two famous 'baths' towns were anciently known as Aquae Sulis and Aquae Arnemetiae for the two goddesses presiding over the hot springs. As Arthur is made out to be the preeminent Christian hero, who in the Welsh Annals has a shield bearing the Cross of Christ that he carries during the Battle of Badon, it would not do for the ancient Romano-British name to be used in this context. To have done so would inevitably have referred directly to a pagan deity. Hence the generic and less "connotation-loaded" Germanic name for the place was substituted. This explanation might do much to placate those who insist on seeing Badon as a Celtic name.

And where is the most likely location for the monte/montis of the Baths/Batham/Badon, where the actual battle was fought?

I make this out to be what is now referred to as The Slopes, at the foot of which is the modern St. Ann's Well, and the Crescent, under which the original Roman bath was built. The Slopes were once called St. Ann's Cliff because it was a prominent limestone outcrop. The Tithe map of 1848 shows that the upper half of the Cliff was still largely covered in trees. I suspect the spring was anciently thought to arise from inside the Cliff, and that the trees covering it marked the precincts of the nemeton or sacred grove of Arnemetia.

The three days and three nights Arthur bore the cross (or, rather, a shield bearing an image of a cross) at Badon in the Welsh Annals are markedly similar to the three days and three nights Urien is said to have blockaded the Saxons in the island of Lindsfarne (British Metcaud) in Chapter 63 of the HB. In Gildas, immediately before mention of Badon, we have the following phrase: "From then on victory went now to our countrymen, now to their enemies..." Similarly, just prior mention of Urien at Lindisfarne, we have this: "During that time, sometimes the enemy, sometimes the Cymry were victorious..." It would seem, therefore, that either the motif of the three days and three nights was taken from the Urien story and inserted into that of Arthur or vice-versa.

What is fascinating about this parallel is that Lindisfarne or 'Holy Island', as it came to be known, was an important spiritual centre of Northern Britain. The inclusion of the three days and three nights (an echo of the period Christ spent in the tomb) in the Badon story suggests that we can no longer accept the view that Arthur's portage of Christian symbols at Badon was borrowed solely from the Castle Guinnion battle account in the HB. Aquae Arnemetiae, like Lindisfarne, was a holy place. Arthur's fighting there may have been construed as a holy act.

Supposedly, 960 Saxons were slain by Arthur at Badon. In the past, most authorities have seen in the number 960 no more than a fanciful embellishment on the Annals' entry, i.e. more evidence of Arthur as a 'legend in the making'. But 960 could be a very significant number, militarily speaking. The first cohort of a Roman legion was composed of six doubled centuries or 960 men. As the most important unit, the first cohort guarded the Roman Imperial eagle standard.

Now, while the Roman army in the late period no longer possessed a first cohort composed of this number of soldiers, it is possible Nennius's 960 betrays an antiquarian knowledge of earlier Roman military structure. However, why the Saxons are said to have lost such a number cannot be explained in terms of such an anachronistic description of a Roman unit.

The simplest explanation for Nennius's 960 is that it represents 8 Saxon long hundreds, each long hundred being composed of 120 warriors.
To quote from Tacitus on the Germanic long hundred:

"On general survey, their [the German's] strength is seen to lie rather in their infantry, and that is why they combine the two arms in battle. The men who they select from the whole force and station in the van are fleet of foot and fit admirably into cavalry action. The number of these chosen men is exactly fixed. A hundred are drawn from each district, and 'the hundred' is the name they bear at home. What began as a mere number ends as a title of distinction"
[Germania 6]

Curiously, in the Norse poem Grimnismal, 8 hundreds of warriors (probably 960) pass through each of the doors of Valhall, the Hall of the Slain, at the time of Ragnarok or the Doom of the Powers.

Osla or Ossa Big-Knife and Caer Faddon

It has often been said that the Welsh Caer Faddon is always a designation for Bath in Avon.

THE ARTHUR OF HISTORY

However, at least one medieval Welsh tale points strongly towards the 'Baths' at Buxton as the proper site.

I am speaking, of course, of the early Arthurian romance 'The Dream of Rhonabwy', sometimes considered to be a part of the Mabinogion collection of tales. Rhonabwy is transported back in time via the vehicle of a dream to the eve of the battle of Caer Faddon. Arthur has apparently come from Cornwall (as he is said to return thither after a truce is made) to mid-Wales and thence to Caer Faddon to meet with Osla or Ossa, a true historical contemporary of Arthur who lies at the head of the royal Bernician pedigree.

As Arthur is said to progress from Rhyd-y-Groes to Long Mountain, he is traveling to the northeast via the Roman road. In other words, he is headed in the direction of Buxton in the High Peak.

While the romance is entirely fanciful, the chronological accuracy in the context of choosing Osla/Ossa is rather uncanny. Furthermore, it is quite clear that in the tradition the author of the romance was drawing from, Caer Faddon is most certainly not Bath. Ossa is known in En lish sources for being the first of the Bernicians\ to come to England from the Continent. Under his descendants, Bernicia became a great kingdom, stretching eventually from the Forth to the Tees. In the 7th century, Deira – which controlled roughly the area between the Tees and the Humber - was joined with Bernicia to form the Kingdom of Northumbria.

In its heyday, Northumbria shared a border with its neighbor to the south – Mercia – at the River Mersey of 'Boundary River'. The Mersey flows east to Stockport, where it essentially starts at the confluence of the River Tame and Goyt. The Goyt has its headwaters on Axe Edge, only a half a dozen kilometers from Buxton in the High Peak.

If we allow for the story's author to have properly chosen Ossa as Arthur's true contemporary, but to have views Northumbria in an anachronistic fashion – i.e. as extending to the River Mersey – then Ossa coming from Bernicia in the extreme north of England, and Arthur coming from Cornwall in the extreme southwest, coming together for a battle at Buxton makes a great deal of sense. In fact, Buxton is pretty much exactly equidistant between the two locations.

Ossa would have been viewed as engaging in a battle just across the established boundary.

If I am right about this, the Welsh knew of the 'Bathum' or Badon that was Buxton.

The Thirteenth Battle: Camlann

After these many victories, Arthur is said to have perished with Medraut at a place called Camlann.

Camlann has long been linked with Camboglanna, the 'Crooked Bank', a Roman fort towards the western end of Hadrian's Wall. The only other candidates for Camlann are in NW Wales (the Afon Gamlan and two other Camlanns near Dolgellau), and these do not have anything to do with the Northern Arthur. For what looks to be a relocation of Arthur to a Camlan in NW Wales, see Appendix III.

Crawford pointed out that the best etymology for Camlann would actually be B. *Cambolanda, 'Crooked Enclosure', an utterly unknown name, but Jackson had no problem with the derivation from Camboglanna.

Those who point to Camelon on the Antonine Wall are ignorant of the fact that this place was originally called Carmuirs. It was renamed Camelodunum in 1526 by the antiquarian Hector Boece. He did this because the Camelon fort has been identified with the Colania of Ptolemy and the Ravenna Cosmography. Colania was confused with Colonia or Colchester, itself called Camulodunum.

The Castlesteads fort sits on a high bluff overlooking the Cambeck valley and the break on the mosses to the north-west which carries the modern road from Brampton to Longtown. The site was drastically leveled in 1791, when the gardens of Castlesteads House were laid out and today nothing is visible of the fort aprt from the southern edge of the fort platform, while the view described above is obscured by trees. The Cam Beck has so far eroded the north-west front of the fort that the side gates now lie only 50 ft from the edge of the gorge. From east to west the fort measures 394 ft and it is thought to have been originally about 400 ft square, covering some 3.75 acres, though it is not impossible that the fort faced south rather than north and was therefore somewhat larger.

Excavations in 1934 revealed the east, west and south walls of the fort, the east and west doubleportal gates and south-west angle tower. The gate towers were built one course deeper than the fort wall, whose foundations were the normal 6 ft wide. All walls had been heavily robbed, but roof-tiles occurred in a number of the towers at ground-floor level, suggesting the possibility of oven-bases, as at Birdoswald, rather than collapsed roofs. Space allowed only for the identification of one ditch, 16 ft wide. No contact has been made with any internal building, but an external bath-house was located and partly dug in 1741.

Castlesteads is unique along the whole Wall for sitting between the Wall and Vallum but not being attached to the former; presumably either its pre-existence or the lie of the land dictated its location.

A carved stone dated roughly 466-599 CE was found at Castlesteads. Because in the past the inscription has been read wrongly, i.e. upside down as 'BEDALTOEDBOS', this has been considered a corrupt attempt at the divine name BELATUCADROS, altars to whom were found here in a Roman context.

However, I have parsed the inscription as actually reading 'SUB DEO LAUDIB[US]', which according to Professor David Howlett of Oxford can be translated as 'with the accompaniment of praises of God'. Thus this stone clearly denotes a Christian presence at Castlesteads during the time of Arthur.

In fact, this area may have been a Christian center during the generation preceding that of Arthur (see the note on the home of St. Patrick in Chapter 5 below).

The Name Medraut/Modred (= Mordred)

On February 26, 1996, I received a letter from Professor Oliver Padel of Cambridge. This was in response to a query I had sent him some time earlier in which I proposed that the name Medrawt – born by the personage who died with Arthur at Camlann – may represent the Roman name Moderatus. What Padel had to say on this possibility is important enough for Arthurian studies to be reprinted in full below:

"Not much has been done on the name of Medrawt or Mordred... In an article on various words in Welsh with the root med, Medr-, Ifor Williams suggested that the name might be connected with the Welsh verb medru 'to be able, to hit'; but he did not develop the idea, only mentioned it in passing.

Middle Welsh Medrawt cannot formally be identical with Old Cornish Modred, Old Breton Modrot (both of which are recorded, indicating an original Old Co.Br. *Modrod), since the Welsh e in the first syllable should not be equivalent to a Co.Br. o there.

What people do not seem to have asked is what this discrepancy means: we can hardly say that Welsh Medrawt is a different name, since it clearly belongs to the same character as Geoffrey's [Geoffrey of Monmouth] Modredus < Co.Br. Modrod.

Which is 'right'? I would suggest that the Co.Br. form is the ancient one, and that the Welsh form has been altered, perhaps indeed by association with the verb medru.

That was already my conclusion, but I did not have a derivation for Modrod. However, Modrod would be the exact derivative of Latin Moderatus, as you suggest. Your suggestion is most attractive, and neither I nor (so far as I know) anyone else has previously thought of it.

Like you, I should be relucatant to say that Modrod couldn't have a Celtic derivation; but it fits so well with Moderatus that I personally don't feel the need to look further."

If Medrawt or, rather, Modrod, is Moderatus, this may be significant for a Medraut at Cambloglanna on Hadrian's Wall, for we know of a Trajanic period prefect named C. Rufius Moderatus, who left inscriptions at Greatchesters on the Wall and Brough-under-Stainmore in Cumbria (CIL iii. 5202, RIB 1737, 166-9, 2411, 147-51). The name of this prefect could have become popular in the region and might even have still been in use among Northern British noble families in the 6th century CE.

Conclusion: Arthur's Military Role in the North

While some of the Arthurian battle sites as I have identified them must be considered problematic or even doubtful, there is no denying that when they are plotted out on a map (see p. 12 above) they stretch from south to north in a fairly well-defined line. Many center on the Roman Dere Street, which must be considered a sort of boundary or frontier zone between the Britons and their enemy, the Germanic invaders.

A battle at Camboglanna does indeed look like an internal conflict, and the tradition which records Medrawt/Moderatus as Arthur's opponent may, in fact, be correct.

To summarize, I include here Alan James' opinion of my Arthurian battle map, found at the beginning of this book:

"If you're assuming late 5th century, the archaelogical and (earliest OE) p-n evidence suggests the main concentration of Germanic-speakers would have been around the Humber, with control of York and extending west to the Magnesian Limestone/ Dere Street - i.e. the beginnngs of Deira and Lindsey; smaller but significant settlements along the Tees, and in the Yorkshire Gap, with control of Catterick; likewise along the Tyne and eastern part of Hadrian's Wall. Further north probably still P-Celtic, but there were of course strategic sites on both sides of the Forth; likewise to the west, strategic sites along the Wall and either side of the Solway Firth.

Whether or not Arthur was involved, I can well believe there were battles at all the places you've marked!"

CHAPTER 4

ARTHUR'S OTHER BATTLES: MYTHOLOGICAL OR MISTAKEN

The Pa Gur Battle Sites

The Arthur presented to us in the early Welsh poem Pa Gur is a very different personage from the one we find in the battle list of Nennius' HB. In Pa Gur, Arthur numbers among his men the mythological Manawyd(an) son of Llyr. He and his men fight monsters and witches. We have clearly departed from history and have embraced the realm of the fantastic.

While the Pa Gur is, alas, a fragmentary poem, the following battles or locations are listed in the order in which they occur.

Elei

Tryfrwyd

Din Eidyn

Celli

Afarnach's hall

Dwellings of Dissethach

Din Eidyn

Shore of Tryfrwyd

Upland of Ystawingun

Mon

Elei is known to be the Ely River in southern Wales. I will treat more of this place in Chapter 6, where its relationship with Campus Elleti will be explored in detail.

I have proposed above that Traeth Tryfrwyd is the shore of the trajectus at Queensferry west of Edinburgh.

Din Eidyn, as is well known, is Edinburgh. Arthur's opponents in this battle are the Cynbyn or 'Dog-heads', whom I believe to be an echo of the Venicones tribe.

Afarnach's hall may be a reference to the Pictish capital of Abernethy. Watson discussed the etymology of Abernethy as follows:

"Thus Abur-nethige of the Pictish Chronicle, now Abernethy near Perth, has as its second part the Genitive of a nominative Nethech or Neitheach (fem.), which is Gaelicized either from Neithon directly, or from a British river name from the same root."

Witches Hole is a small cave in a rocky face on the north side of the Castle Law fort at Abernethy. It is supposed to have been the residence of some of the Witches of Abernethy (http://canmore.rcahms.gov.uk/en/site/27921/details/witches+hole+castle+law/).

I would add that Neithon comes from an original Nechtan or Neachtan, which appears to be cognate with L. Neptune.

Abernethy is on the border region between the Pictish kingdoms of Fortriu and Circenn. We have seen above that the Dalriadan Arthur is said to have fought in Circenn, and the Abernethy/Afarnach battle may well be a traditional memory of the Circenn conflict.

If Afarnach is Abernethy, we may presume that Celli, the 'Grove', was to be found somewhere in the region that stretched between Edinburgh and Abernethy. Unfortunately, there are many Gaelic grove place-names (coille and variants) as well as English place-name elements with similar meanings in this part of central Scotland, so it may well prove impossible to locate the Celli where Cai is said to have fought. As its being lost is emphasized in the poem (Pan colled kelli, 'when lost was Celli'), we must assume it was a place of some importance.

I would very tentatively put forward a connection between Celli, 'Grove', and the Medionemeton or 'Middle Sacred Grove' mentioned in the Ravenna Cosmography. The Ravenna Cosmography situates the Medionemeton between the entries for the 'Camelon' Roman fort and the Ardoch Roman fort, and this would accord well with a Celli between Edinburgh and Abernethy. To date, two proposed identifications for the nemeton have been offered: Cairnpapple in West Lothian and the Arthur's Oven shrine which once stood near Larbert, a town across the Carron River from

Camelon. Arthur's Oven is almost certainly the structure mentioned in the HB of Nennius:

Chapter 23: "The Emperor Carausius rebuilt it [the Antonine Wall] later, and fortified it with seven forts, between the two estuaries, and a Round House of polished stone, on the banks of the river Carron..."

Dissethach, where Arthur's opponent is Pen Palach, looks like Tig Scathach, 'House of Scathach', and Beinn na Caillich (allowing for the difference between P- and Q- Celtic), 'Hill of the Witch'. Dunsgiath or Dun Scathach, the 'Fort of Scathach', and Beinn na Caillich, are both in the southeast of the Isle of Skye. From Beatrix Faerber, CELT project manager, we learn that there is a reference in Tochmarc Emire, which incorporates the story of Cu Chulainn's training at arms with Scathach. In this case, Scathach's house is tig Scathgi (= Schathaigi).

The upland of (Y)stawingun, where nine witches are slain by Cei, is quite possibly Stanton Moor in Derbyshire, where we find the stone circle called the Nine Ladies. The 'lord of Emrys' mentioned in the poem just prior to (Y)stawingun is a known periphrasis for Gwynedd, as Ambrosius/Emrys was the traditional lord of that land. Emrys in this context may actually be a reference to the Amber river, which lies just east of Stanton Moor.

The –gun, if from an earlier –cun, could have come about by mistaking in MS. an original t for

c. The middle –w– may represent a u, such as is found in Staunton, a known variant of Stanton.

Much later story substitutes the hero Peredur and transplants the witches to Gloucester, presumably because of the presence in Gloucestershire of towns named Stanton and Staunton.

There is no mystery regarding Mon, as this is the common Welsh name for the Isle of Anglesey in northwest Wales. Welsh tradition insists that Cath Palug or Cath Palug, which Cai battles on Mon, is the cat of a person called Palug. Modern scholars prefer to view palug as perhaps meaning 'scratching' or 'clawing', hence Cath Palug as the Clawing Cat.

Cath Palug is linked in line 82 of the poem to 'lleuon', i.e. lions. The association of lions with Arfon (where the cat is born) and Mon may have to do with the simple confusion of llew, 'lion', for lleu, the god who is the Lord of Gwynedd in Welsh tradition. The letters u and w readily substitute for each other.

Two Additional Poetic References

Much has been made of early references to Arthur in three important poems: The Gododdin, Marwnad Cynddylan and Geraint son of Erbin. As I have discussed The Gododdin reference already above (Chapter 3) in the context of Arthur's battle at Mount Agned, here I will restrict myself to a brief treatment of the other two poems.

MARWNAD CYNDDYLAN

Scholar Jenny Rowland has done a very nice job of disposing of the difficulty posed by Line 46 of Marwnad Cynddylan. The line in question reads:

Canawon artir wras dinas degyn

This has in the past been amended to read:

Canawon Arthur wras dinas degyn: "whelps of Arthur, a resolute protection"

Jenny Rowland, wisely, opts instead for:

Canawon artir[n]wras dinas degyn, i.e.: Canawon arddyrnfras dinas degyn: "strong-handed whelps..."

This nicely eliminates our having to associate Arthur with the Powys kingdom in east-central Wales.

GERAINT SON OF ERBIN

A harder thing to dispose of is the presence of Arthur's name in the poem Geraint son of Erbin. While different versions of the poem exist, all are in agreement in including the name Arthur in one of their stanzas. This would not be a problem, were it not for the fact that, in Jenny Rowland's words, "Despite the Arthurian link in Geoffrey of Monmouth's work there can be no question that 'Geraint fab Erbin' is older than the Historia Regum Britanniae." In other words, someone, for some reason, seems to have placed Arthur in Dumnonia (Devon and Cornwall) prior to Geoffrey of Monmouth's doing so.

If, as is genuinely agreed, Geraint son of Erbin is to be dated between the ninth and eleventh centuries, how do we account for Arthur being in Dumnonia? This is a critical question, for Geraint son of Erbin would seem to be our earliest source seeking to situate Arthur in extreme southwest England.

Using Rowland's composite text, I can make the following observations: Geraint's name occurs in 18 out of 27 stanzas. To these we may add a 19th stanza containing 'the son of Erbin'. Other than the names of Geraint and Erbin, and the single occurrence of the name of Arthur, there are no other personal names in the poem.

Also, it is suspicious that Arthur's name is used in exactly the same way as is that of Geraint. The variants of the 'Arthurian' line are as follows:

"En Llogporth y gueleise Arthur... En llogporth y gueleise y Arthur... Yn llongborth llas y Arthur..."

Professor Patrick Sims-Williams has suggested that to solve the problem posed by the 'syntactically and semantically ambiguous' y before Arthur's name that this line be considered 'a poetic inversion' for 'men to (i.e. vassals of) Arthur', the 'men' in question being the warriors of the following line:

Gwyr dewr kymynynt a/o dur; "brave men, they hewed with steel"

The Red Book of Hergest has instead: "In Llongborth Arthur lost brave men, they hewed with steel"

Of course, the y is in front of Arthur's name even in the Red Book version. The odd thing about the poem is that Geraint's name is used in exactly the same context. We have the Black Book of Carmarthen's:

En Llogporth y llas y Gereint...

Which is, however, rendered in the Red Book of Hergest as

En Llogporth y llas Gereint...

The cumulative effect of the panegyric, with its formulaic repetition of Geraint's name, and the sudden intrusion of Arthur's within the same cymeriad, is designed to enable us to see Arthur in this context not as a separate individual, but as an honorific being applied to Geraint.

In other words, just as we find a warrior in The Gododdin compared unfavorably to Arthur, who is there decidedly a famous figure of the past, in the Geraint fab Erbin elegy the heroic nature of Geraint is so great during the Llongporth battle that he symbolically is Arthur, the 'emperor' and 'ruler of battle'.

THE ARTHUR OF HISTORY

Those who attempt to account for Arthur's presence in the poem have in the past resorted to two explanations. First, that Arthur really was there, which would put this particular Geraint back in Arthur's time, or that a warrior troop whose predecessors had served under Arthur was still, in Geraint's day, referred to as 'Arthur's men'.

There are two problems with these explanations. In the first case, it seems fairly certain that the Llongporth battle is to be identified with the battle fought at Langport by the Wessex chieftains Ine and Nunna against a Dumnonian Geraint in c. 710. This event is memorialized in the ASC, where it is described as a Saxon victory. Needless to say, the 8th century is well outside the time period of Arthur.

That the men fighting with Geraint are composed of a troop whose members originally flocked to Arthur's standard makes little sense, given that the same 'brave men' (gwyr dewr) are ascribed to Geraint:

"In Llongborth Geraint lost [or 'I saw to'] Brave men from the region of Dyfnaint. And before they were killed, they killed."

In following Geraint, these warriors were fighting for a chieftain who in the praise language of the poem was an incarnation of Arthur. While it could be argued that Geraint's fighting alongside Arthur or the latter's men might be considered praise enough, from the perspective of the panegyrist, whose sole goal was to glorify Geraint, to use Arthur or his men in this fashion would actually have diminished Geraint's stature. Why would a poet seeking to praise Geraint distract his audience by calling attention to the presence of another, greater hero?

We need only ask this final question: who is greater, a Geraint who by virtue of his martial prowess is literally an Arthur, or a Geraint who needs the help of Arthur and/or Arthur's men in battle?

The Three Prisons of Arthur

Triad 52 of the Triads of the Island of Britain concerns itself with the 'Three Exalted Prisoners of the Island of Britain'. After listing the three prisoners, the Triad continues as follows:

"And one [prisoner], who was more exalted than the three of them, was three nights in prison in CAER OETH AND ANOETH, and three nights imprisoned by GWEN PENDRAGON, and three nights in an enchanted prison under the STONE OF ECHYMEINT [Llech Echemeint]. This exalted prisoner was Arthur."

Can we identify these prisons and Gwen Pendragon with known places or personages? Might they have had something to do with the Arthurian battle sites?

Gwen Pendragon has not been identified in the past. Gwen is the feminine form of Gwyn and means 'the white or fair one' (later, the 'blessed one'). It is possible that here Gwen is being used as an eponym for the Guinnion of Castellum Guinnion, an Arthurian battle site in Nennius. Guinnion derives from the same word meaning 'white' plus a locative suffix akin to Latin -ium. As the "holy" Mary is carried on Arthur's shield during this battle, it is not inconceivable that 'Gwen' is a reference to Mary, and that Guinnion itself is being thought of as being named for her.

However, given that one of the famous dragons of Dinas Emrys was white, we should perhaps interpret Gwen as the genius of the Saxons. This white dragon was found by Emrys (or Ambrosius, later identified wrongly by Geoffrey of Monmouth with Myrddin/Merlin) in a subterranean context. This monster's companion in the 'Otherworld' below Dinas Emrys was the red dragon, the genius of the British people. It is my guess that here Arthur is being identified with the red dragon, buried in the prison of the white 'chief dragon', a comparable leader of the Saxons.

According to Geoffrey of Monmouth, both Ambrosius, uncle of Arthur, and Uther, Arthur's father, were buried at Stonehenge next to Amesbury, ancient Ambresbyrig, a site confused in the tradition with Dinas Emrys. Arthur placed in a typical 'death-prison' at Stonehenge with his father and uncle may preserve an otherwise lost Welsh tradition which runs counter to the more popular one situating him at Avalon. In passing, I should mention that the white and red dragons are also placed in a pit at Oxford in the MABINOGION tale "Lludd and Llevelys." Oxford is there claimed as the center of Britain, and the

Rollright Stones may be the local substitute for Stonehenge.

The Llech or Stone of Echemeint would appear to be a reference to Bath, which the Welsh identified with Arthur's Mount Badon. According to the ASC (year entry 973 CE), Bath was also known by the name Acemannes-ceaster. This alternate name for Bath appears to be a development from the ancient Romano-British names for the town, Aquae Sulis and Aquae Calidae.

And what about Caer Oeth and Anoeth? Oeth means 'something difficult to obtain or achieve, a difficulty, a wonder; something strange or wonderful'. Anoeth has essentially the same meaning, as the prefix an- is merely an intensifier: 'a wonder, something difficult to acquire; something strange or difficult'.

The Caer Oeth and Anoeth placename is also mentioned in the Mabinogion tale Culhwch and Olwen, where it is one of the castles Arthur boasts of gaining entrance to. Once again, in the Stanzas of the Graves we are told that the burial ground of the host of Caer Oeth and Anoeth can be found in Gwanas near Cadair Idris in Ceredigion.

Gwanas is very near the Camlans of Merionethshire. In fact it is exactly between the Afon Gamlan to the northwest and the other two Camlans to the east and southeast. This can hardly be coincidence and probably indicates the "wonderful" grave for Arthur near the fatal battle site, which Welsh tradition (see Appendix III) relocates to NW Wales.

In the Welsh 'Stanzas of the Graves', we are told 'anoeth bin u bedd arthur'. This has been translated in various ways. But some (myself included) have noticed that anoeth in this line may be an oblique reference to both the teulu (house-hold warriors) of oeth and anoeth and Cair ('fort') Oeth and Anoeth. In Triad 52 we are told Arthur was a prisoner in Caer Oeth and Anoeth.

We know where a military force from Caer Oeth and Anoeth ended up: Gwanas, a mountainous region situated exactly between the Welsh Camlanns. They had gone there in order to rob the rich graves of, we must presume, their "anoetheu" or "wonders."

A detailed investigation of the Gwanas region reveals an interesting candidate for the so-called 'beddau hir' or long graves of the place. The best account of this candidate is found on the COFLEIN site:

"A small square earthwork set upon a ridge summit has been identified as a possible Roman military tower. It is set on the crest of a south-facing ridge, commanding extensive views across the upland basin below Pen-y-Brynnfforchog and the course of the Roman road between Caer Gai and Brithdir.

A range of alternative interpretations can be advanced, notably that this is a Roman or early

Medieval square ditched barrow, such as are found at Druid beyond Bala (NPRN 404711), and Croes Faen near Tywyn (NPRN 310263). As such it would, with Tomen-y-Mur (NPRN 89420), be a rare surviving earthwork example, most sites being known only from cropmarks. This monument might be compared to the small practice work at Llyn Hiraethllyn (NPRN 89703), otherwise the smallest example of its type known in Wales.

It is a square platform about 5.0m across with a shallow ditch up to 2.8m across on the south-east, 1.1m wide on the north-east and south-west and not discernable on the north-west. The platform has low banks on the north-east and south-west sides. As a Roman work the earthwork has been associated with a road or track passing below the ridge to the south-east (NPRN 91903), suggested as part of the Roman road between Caer Gai and Brithdir (Rigg & Toller 1983, 165; Britannia XXVIII (1997), 399), although this has been disputed as it is a modern feature (Browne 1986) and is depicted on the 1st edition OS 1" map of 1837 (sheet 59 north-east). A tower on this site would command extensive views of the tributary valley to the south-east, but not of the main Wnion valley on the north-west and the Brithdir military settlement (NPRN 95480) may be out of sight. The earthwork is intervisible with the 'Rhyd Sarn' works 11.5km to the north-east towards Bala Lake (NPRN 303162-3)."

The 'low banks' of this monument (if that is what it really is!) nicely answer for the 'long graves' of Gwanas.

THE ARTHUR OF HISTORY

There are no other candidates for the beddau hir. Of course, time and the combined ravages of Man and Nature may long since have destroyed any other such monuments in the region.

But what of Caer Oeth and Anoeth itself? The site has not been identified.

I think, though, that the clue is in the name. Rachel Bronwich in her TRIADS suggests that the fortress was "of difficult access", which is one possible meaning of the word oeth. Anoeth would in this context merely have an amplified sense. But the important thing to remember here is that anoeth could be a wonderful, strange treasure or Otherworld object. Or the word can refer to the process of obtaining such an object, this being a difficult task to accomplish. Such is made plain in the MABINOGION story "Culhwch and Olwen." Fiona Dehghani discusses anoetheu in her article "The Anoetheu Dialogue in Culhwch ac Olwen" (Proceedings of the Harvard Celtic Colloquium, Vol. 26/27 (2006/2007), pp. 291-305). Other scholars have discussed the word at some length, including Rachel Bromwich in the notes to her TRIADS.

Arthur is released from the prison of Caer Oeth and Anoeth by one Goreu son of Custennin, who plays an important role in "Culhwch and Olwen." I believe this point has been overlooked. There is even a point near the end of the tale in which Culhwch and Goreu return to the castle of Ysbaddaden the Giant with the anoetheu.

Goreu slays the giant and Culhwch takes the fort, marring the giant's daughter, Olwen. There is no mention of the anoetheu (here the objects of the difficult tasks the giant had laid upon Culhwch) leaving the place.

It seems fairly obvious to me, therefore, that Ysbaddaden's castle is Caer Oeth and Anoeth. This is the only fort of anoetheu that we know of, and the only one directly involving Arthur and his men. It is true that Arthur and his warriors raid various Otherworld castles in the poem "The Spoils of Annwm", but these actions are not defined as anoetheu and we are not told of a castle where stolen Otherworld objects are stored.

Can we determine where Caer Oeth and Anoeth is located? I believe we can. If the fort is, in fact, that of Ysbaddaden, I successfully identified the site years ago (see my book THE MYSTERIES OF AVALON). It is none other than The Wrekin hillfort in Shropshire.

Wrekin is a form of the Romano-British name Viroconium (see Rivet and Smith's THE PLACE-NAMES OF ROMAN BRITAIN for an extensive discussion of the various forms). The Romans built the city of Viroconium after they had destroyed the hillfort of the Cornovii.

CHAPTER 5

THE NORTHERN KINGDOMS

To give some idea of the political landscape of Arthur's Britain, it might be helpful to examine some of the "Men of the North" and the kingdoms they controlled.

The most northern of these kingdoms was, of course, the ancient territory of the Votadini or Gododdin, which in the Roman period is believed to have stretched from the Wear or the Tyne through Northumberland and the Lothians to the Forth.

The term 'Lothian' appears to have been of Dark Age origin, which as we have seen stands for an original Lleudiniawn, 'Place of the Fort of [the god] Lugus'. There is an eponymous king recorded in the Life of St. Kentigern called Leudonus, i.e. Lleuddun, and his kingdom in Welsh was known as Lleuddunion. He was supposed to have ruled from Traprain Law, which was earlier called Dunpelder, the 'Fort of the Spear (shaft)'.

In the late 6th century, the king of the Votadini was, apparently, one Mynyddog Mwynfawr. He is said to have ruled from Din Eidyn or Edinburgh and was the son of a certain Ysgyran, and probably succeeded Clydno Eidyn. The Gododdin poem implies that the Britons who fought the English at Cattraeth assembled at Mynyddog's court at Edinburgh. Clydno Eidyn, in turn, was the son of Cynfelyn son of Dyfnwal Hen. Myynyddog is also given the epithet 'Eidyn' meaning, undoubtedly, 'of Eithne'. Once again, Eidyn is likely the British form of Eithne, mother of the god Lugh in Irish tradition.

Pabo Post Prydain, the 'Pillar of Britain', is the son of Ceneu son of Coel Hen, both famous chieftains of the North. Pabo is spelled Pappo in the genealogies appended to the HB. Coel Hen's name is believed to be preserved in Kyle in Ayreshire.

A son of Pabo is Dunod Fwr, who is probably the chieftain who fought against the Rheged princes in Erechwydd, which itself is usually placed somewhere in Cumbria. We may relate this Dunod to Dent in NorthWest Yorkshire, his lands here being termed the 'regio Dunotinga', kingdom of the descendents of Dunod. From John Morris's The Age of Arthur:

"DENT: regio Dunotinga is one of four districts of north-western Yorkshire overrun by the English in or before the 670s, Eddius 17 [Life of Wilfrid]. The passage is overlooked in EPNS WRY 6, 252, where the early spellings Denet(h) are rightly related to a British Dinned or the like, and Ekwall's derivation from a non-existent British equivalent of the Old Irish dind, hill, is properly dismissed. EPNS does not observe that Dent was, and still is, the name of a considerable region, and tha thte village is still locally known as Dent Town, in contrast with the surrounding district of Dent.... Regio Dunotinga plainly takes its name from a person named Dunawt, Latin Donatus, as does the district of Dunoding in

Merioneth, named from another Dunawt, son of Cunedda."

The regio Dunotinga was associated with the Ribble and other places in the north of the West Riding. As the Dent River is a tributary of the upper Lune in Lonsdale, and Upper Lonsdale seems to have been within the canton of the ancient Carvetii tribe, it is likely that Dunot was himself descended from the 'People of the Stag'. The Carvetii (see Cerwyd/Cerwydd below) ruled over what we now think of as Cumbria and adjacent areas.

Bran son of Ymellyrn is associated with both Dunawt of Dent and Cynwyd of Kent (see below for the Cynwydion). The patronymic here is transparently from Old Norse a, river, plus melr, sandbank, identifying his region with Ambleside in Cumbria just to the west of the River Kent.

Another son of Pabo's is Cerwyd or Cerwydd, who is otherwise completely unknown. This name is transparently an eponym for the Carvetii tribe. We have just seen that Dunod's Dent seems to have been a part of the territory once covered by this ancient tribal kingdom.

The form Cerwydd as a direct eponym for the Carvetii is not possible; we would need Cerwyd for an exact linguistic correspondence. However, as Cerwydd means 'stag-like one', we can say with a fair degree of certainty that he does represent the People of the Stag.

As for Pabo, father of Dunod, we may situate him at Papcastle (Pabecastr in 1260), the Derventio Roman fort in Cumbria. Pap- is thought to be from ON papa, papi, for 'hermit', but this seems an unlikely name for a 'ceaster'. Instead we should look to early W. pab, 'pope', i.e. papa, pl. pabeu, and Llanbabo church of St. Pabo in Anglesey. Pabo's Chester would seem to do quite nicely. We could then locate Pabo within the Carvetii kingdom of his sons Cerwyd/Cerwydd and Dunod.

I would add that Pabo's epithet 'Post' or 'Pillar' is possibly a reference to the Solway, which is believed to be from OScand. sul, 'pillar or post', and vath, 'ford'. It has been proposed, quite reasonably I think, that the pillar or post of the Solway is the Lochmaben Stone at Gretna Green. A 'papa' or 'father' of the post/pillar named for the Divine Son Mabon makes for an interesting combination of place-name elements!

However, it is true that the Papcastle fort is not on the Solway. The name of the Roman period fort here – Derventio – was named for the river Derwent, the 'oak-river' or 'river in an oakwood'. As the oak was a very sacred tree to the early Celts, it is possible the 'post' or 'pillar' that gave its name to Pabo was an oaken one and thus an indirect reference to the place-name.

Sawyl Benisel ("Low-head"), yet another son of Pabo, is dated c. 480 CE. On the Ribble, not far south of 'regio Dunotinga', is a town called Samlesbury. The place-name expert Eilert Ekwall has Samlesbury as 'Etymology obscure', but then proposes OE sceamol, 'bench', as its first element, possibly in the topographical sense of 'ledge'. A.D. Mills follows Ekwall by saying that this place-name is probably derived from scamol plus burh (dative byrig). However, sceamol/scamol is not found in other place-names where a 'ledge' is being designated. Instead, the word scelf/scielf/scylfe, 'shelf of level or gently sloping ground, ledge' is used.

I would suggest as a better etymology for Samlesbury: 'Sawyl's fort'. There are, for example, Sawyl place-names in Wales (Llansawel, Pistyll Sawyl, now Ffynnon Sawyl). Sawyl is the Welsh form of the name Samuel.

Dr. Andrew Breeze of Pamplona, a noted expert on British place-names, agrees with this proposed etymology:

"I feel sure you are right. The form surely contains the Cumbric equivalent of Welsh _Sawyl_<_Samuel_. Your explanation of this toponym in north Lancashire is thus new evidence for Celtic survival in Anglo-Saxon times."

Now that we have placed Pabo and his descendents on the map, we need to investigate what has been explained as an intrusion on their pedigree.

An Arthwys and his father Mar are both inserted into the Pabo genealogy. Instead of Pabo son of Ceneu son of Coel Hen, we have Pabo son of Arthwys son of Mar son of Ceneu, etc. This same Arthwys is made the grandfather of a Cynwyd of the tribal group known as the Cynwydion (of the Kent river in Cumbria - Kent being from Kennet, which in Welsh is Cynwyd), of Gwenddolau of Carwinley (Caer Gwenddolau just a little north of Carlisle) and father of Eliffer (Eleutherius) of York. Eliffer in another pedigree is the son of Gwrgwst Ledlum (Fergus Mor of Dalriada) son of Ceneu son of Coel Hen.

Mar is made the father of Lleenog, father of Gwallog of the kingdom of Elmet (a small kingdom centreed about Leeds, probably from Welsh elfydd, 'world, land'), but in another pedigree it is Maeswig Gloff, i.e. Maeswig 'the Lame', who is father of Lleenog.

Mar, whose name is also written Mor, is once again Fergus Mor (also spelled ' Fergus Mar'). Proto-Celtic *maro-, 'great', is found in Old Irish as both mar and mor, although in OW this is maur, and in MW mawr.

In the Strathclyde genealogy proper, we find a Garbaniaun son of [Ceneu son of] Coel Hen. This Garbaniaun has a son named Dumngual Moilmut or Dyfnwal Moelmul. Both names are, rather transparently, forms of the Dalriadan prince Gabran (Garbaniaun shows a metathesis of Gabran, plus a territorial suffix, as in Gwrtheyrniaun, a region named for Gwrtheyrn/Vortigern; cf. with Garban for Gabran in the Irish Book of Lecan) and his son Domnall. The Bran son of Dumngual/Domnall of the British pedigree is probably the attested Bran son of Aedan son of Gabran.

I should note that scholars have preferred to see in Garbaniaun the Roman Germanianus. However, Germanianus is a rare Latin name, and why it should have appeared among the Strathclyde Britons at this time is very hard to explain. There was a 4th century Prefect of Gaul bearing this name, but no one else of any note, so far as our records tell us.

While we need not take these apparent intrusions of Irish Dalriadan royal names into the British Strathclyde genealogy at face value, they probably do indicate the existence of marriage ties between the Strathclyde Britons and their neighbors, the Dalriadans. Such marriage ties are hinted at in the records which pertain to the history of Scottish Dalriada (see John Bannerman's Studies in the History of Dalriada, Edinburgh and London, 1974).

Maeswig (Masguic Clop in the Harleian genealogies) as a name appears to be from *Magosvicos, 'Fighter of the Plain'. This may be a reference to the Roman fort at Burrow Walls, Workington, Cumbria, named Magis, "the fossilised Latin locative plural of a name formed on British *magos... The sense then seems to be 'at the plains' (Rivet and Smith)." It is possible Maeswig as 'Plain-fighter' was derived from a tribal designation for a group at the fort called the Magovices, Plain-Fighters or, perhaps, Fighters of Magis.

Other Northern chieftains were likewise placed at Roman forts. Pabo Post Prydain, for example, belongs at Papcastle, west of Burrow Walls on the River Derwent. Magis itself is at the mouth of the same river.

The name Arthwys has frequently been brought into connection with that of Arthur/Artorius. This name is from Arth-, 'Bear', + -wys. Dr. Simon Rodway of The University of Wales tells me that

"There is an element –wys found in a number of words of obscure meaning and derivation which could be present in Arthwys, cf. doublets like mam ~ mamwys, neuadd ~ neuaddwys (Ifor Williams, The Poems of Taliesin, trans. J. E. C. Williams (Dublin, 1968), p. 51)."

Dr. Andrew Breeze has made a case for the river Irthing containing the word Arth, 'bear'. From his article "Celts, Bears and the River Irthing" (Archaeologia Aeliana, 5th series, volume XXXII):

Irthing, which has early forms Irthin, Erthina, and Erthing, would also make sense as 'little bear', with a Cumbric diminutive suffix corresponding to Middle and Modern Welsh –yn (Old Welsh –inn), as in defynyn 'droplet' from dafn 'drop' or mebyn 'young boy' from mab 'boy'. As the th of Arth is pronounced like that of English bath, but that of Irthing like that of brother, the process of voicing here would take place after borrowing by English, not before."

The claim has been made that Arthwys should be Athrwys, as this spelling is found in later sources. The argument would seem to have some support as the name Athrwys is found in

Wales. If it was Athrwys, the first element would be W athro 'teacher' (< PIE *pH2tro:w- 'uncle'). However, as Professor Ranko Matasovic has pointed out to me via private correspondence, while we have plenty of examples of Arth- or bear names, other than the presumed Athrwys, we have absolutely no other extant names containing athro.

[NOTE: Arthwys can be interpreted as a territorial designation, rather than strictly as a personal name. Welsh has a -wys suffix, which derives from Latin –enses. A discussion of this suffix can be found in John T. Koch's Celtic Culture, among other sources. Regedwis, for example, is 'people of Rheged' - or maybe better, 'inhabitants of Rheged'. The entry for -wys (1) in the University of Wales Dictionary confirms it as a Latin borrowing and as a nominal plural ending, giving the examples of Gwennwys, Lloegrwys and Monwys. Could –wys, then, be a suffix used for the people who live on a certain river? Like on an Arth or Bear River?

When I put this question to Dr. Delyth Prys of the place-name experts at The University of Wales, Bangor, he replied: "I've no independent evidence for this, but river names are sometimes used as the name for a more general area and by extension it could be the people of the Arth (area)." Now, if the Irthing is not from ir-t, but from erth/arth +inga (belonging to, not descendents of), it would be the 'tun belonging to Arth' or belonging to the bear. But if the river itself were originally the Arth/Erth, then the tun itself would belong to the river.

Alan James of BLITON states that river-names can sometimes be also the names of adjacent regions, or - probably more correctly - some river-names may have originally have been regional names (or vice versa). This may have been the case with Llwyfenydd/ Lyvennet of Urien. The kind of river-names that seem to double as district names tend to be ones that refer to local terrain, etc., but that may just because such topographical names are more obviously linked to the area. Again, rivers were sometimes boundaries, but they're as likely to flow through a territory perceived as one as to divide such a territory into two. A hypothetical Arth/'Bear' region could have included both the Irt and the Irth of Irthington, not necessarily been bounded by them.]

Arthuret near Carwinley was the scene of a great battle featuring Myrddin, among others. This famous hero (see my THE MYSTERIES OF AVALON) belonged at the twin hills of Ardd Gurrith and Ardd Errith, from which the Arthuret and Arderydd names derive. Arf-derydd, 'weapon fierce', is actually a poetic descriptor for the battle, and Derydd is probably the original British name of the Liddel Water at Carwinley. Dreon son of Nudd, another famous hero at the Arthuret battle, is likely a son of the Nudd mentioned on an early 6th century tombstone at Yarrow Kirk.

Not far west of the Carwinley of Gwenddolau on the coast of Galloway is the fort of Caerlaverock. The name of this fort is referred to in Welsh tradition as the 'Lark's Nest' and it is said to have been the cause of the Battle of Arfderydd (Arthuret). But 'lark' is itself either a mistake or pun for the personal name Llywarch, in this case Llywarch Hen son of Elidir Lydanwyn. Llywarch was first cousin to Urien Rheged. Caerlaverock is, therefore, Caer Llywarch.

There is another interesting reference to a place in Cumbria that I might mention. In the 'Cambridge' group of Historia Brittonum MSS., an interpolation tells us that Vortigern is said to have built "Guasmoric near Carlisle, a city which in English is called Palme castre." Palme castre has long been erroneously identified with the Old Carlisle Roman fort one mile south of Wigton in the parish of Westward. There is a double-error in the Historia Brittonum, for Guasmoric itself is not the same place as the Palme castre fort.

Guasmoric must be Gwas Meurig, the "Abode of Meurig or Mauricius." This is clearly an attempt at rendering the Gabrosentum Roman fort in Cumbria at Moresby. According to both Ekwall and Mills, Moresby (Moriceby, Moresceby) is Maurice's By, Maurice being a Norman name and -by being Old Scandinavian for "farmstead, village, settlement". Whether we can propose an original Welsh Meurig underlying Maurice is questionable. In all likelihood, the interpolation is late and Guasmoric represents Maurice's By. If originally a Meurig place-name, this may commemorate the 6th century Meurig son of Idno son of Meirchion, who married a daughter of Gwallog of Elmet. Cynfarch son of Meirchion may have left his name at the Mote of Mark in Dumfries.

As for Palme castre, this is a place now called Plumpton (Plumton, 'tun where plum trees grow'; see Ekwall) in Cumbria. Directly between Plumpton and Plumpton Foot is the Voreda Roman fort. Rivet and Smith (The Place-Names of Roman Britain) list the fort as being "at Old Penrith, Plumpton Wall, Cumberland, beside the river Petteril". Voreda means 'horse' in British.

As archaeology has shown us, there were two main centres for the Carvetii kingdom. One was the ancient tribal centre near Brougham, the Roman Brocavum, with its triple sacred henges at Eamont. One of these henges is actually called King Arthur's Round Table and another the Little Round Table. There is evidence in the form of a concentration of inscriptions at Brougham that the primary Carvetii deity worshipped at these henges was a horned god (doubtless a stag, given that Carvetii means 'People of the Stag') named Belatucadros.

But there was also an important region called variously Erechwydd or Yr Echwydd, mentioned in connection with Urien, his sons, Gwallog son of Lleenog of Elmet and with Dunod Fwr. No wholly satisfactory identification of Erechwydd has yet been made, but it would seem to be somewhere in or close to Cumbria.

What we do know about Erechwydd is that the Er- prefix is not the definite article yr, even though the name is sometimes wrongly written 'yr echwyd' in the poetry, but a form of Ar-, as found in other place-names, e.g. Arfon. Ar- as a prefix originally meant 'in front of'. But it came to have the senses of 'upon, on, over, at, in, across from'.

The National Dictionary of Wales defines echwydd as 'fresh (of water, as opp. to salt); fresh water'. However, although this meaning has been extrapolated from the contexts in which the word is used, no good etymology had yet been proposed.

I asked Graham Isaac if the word could come from ech, 'out of, from', plus a form of the Indo-European root *ued, 'wet'. His response was:

"The etymology echwydd < *exs-wed-yo-, or *exs-ud-yo- (either would probably do it) seems plausible enough."

The literal meaning would then be the 'out-water', but the sense of the word would be simply 'flowing, fresh water'. Again, the Welsh texts which use this word leave no doubt that we are talking about fresh water emerging from springs or lakes.

So where was Erechwydd/Yr Echewydd, the 'Place by the flowing, fresh water'? Our clue lies not only in the name of the region, but in the battles fought there between Dunod Fwr of the Dent region and Gwallog of Elmet against Urien's sons. These engagements are recounted in the Llywarch Hen poetry. Given that Urien Rheged seems to have had his origin in Galloway (where we find Dun Ragit, the 'Hill-fort of Rheged'), and both Dunod and Gwallog had kingdoms in southeastern Cumbria and just southeast of Cumbria, respectively, the most logical place to seek Erechwydd would be the twin valleys of the Eden and Petteril.

A Roman road led from the south up through the valley of the river Lune right past Dunod's Dentdale. This road continued north to the Eden Valley. Another Roman road led west from Leeds and joined with the Lonsdale road. Gwallog could have taken this route to the Eden or he could have gone north up Dere Street and then cut over through the Pennines at Stainmore.

The Eden and Petteril Valleys were the heartland of the ancient Carvetii kingdom. Not only did the twin valleys provide the obvious natural route from Carlisle towards Lancaster and York, the area has been shown to have supported a widespread and occasionally dense pattern of rural settlement in the Roman period.

It is even possible that Erechwydd as a regional designation can be more precisely localized within the Eden and Petteril Valleys. The headwaters of the Petteril lie just west-northwest of Eamont. We have already discussed the importance of Eamont with its sacred henges. The river Eamont (a back-formation from the name Eamont itself, from AS ea-gemot, 'river-meet', i.e. confluence) and Lowther join at Eamont Bridge and continue for a short distance eastward to the Eden. There was also, of course, a nexus of Roman roads at Eamont.

In my opinion, the Anglo-Saxon place-name ea-gemot/Eamont may overlie an original British Echwydd. Ekwall thought Eamont refers to the confluence of the Eamont and the stream from Dacre, although given the location of the Brougham/Brocavum Roman fort at the juncture of the Eamont and Lowther, it makes much more sense to see this ea-gemot as the confluence of the latter two rivers. If I am right, then Arechwydd was the Eamont area, specifically the land at and around the Brougham fort and the three Carvetii henges. The 'out-water' would be a reference specifically to the Eamont, which is formed by the outflow from the Ullswater, the second largest lake in Cumbria.

Just a few miles south-southest of Eamont is the Lyvennet Beck, a tributary of the Eden. This has been identified with the Llwyfenyd over which Urien is said to have been 'ruler' (Welsh teithiawc).

A Note of Godeu of the North and Urbs Giudi

A very important region in the North of Britain was called Godeu. This place is mentioned in two of the Taliesin praise-poems of Urien. In both cases, Godeu is paired with Reget, i.e. Rheged. Yet Godeu has remained unidentified.

Locating Godeu is complicated by its use in an ancient battle poem called Kat Godeu, the 'Battle of Godeu'. Because this battle poem tells of the god Gwydion's magical activation of an army of trees, it has in the past been assumed that

Godeu meant 'forest', cf. Welsh coed/goed. However, the word godeu or goddeu/goddau actually existed in early Welsh. The National Dictionary of Wales has as the meaning of this word 'intention, design, purpose, object or aim, end in view.'

There are some clues about where we might find the Godeu of Kat Godeu. Firstly, we know Gwydion was most firmly associated with Gwynedd. One other character mentioned in the poem – a certain Peblig, can be put in Gwynedd. The only Peblig known to Welsh tradition was the saint of Llanbeblig, the parish church of Carnarvon. This Peblig is involved in the actual battle in Godeu, at a fort called Caer Nefenhir.

In the Mabinogion tale Math Son of Mathonwy, Gwydion fights Pryderi of Dyfed in Gwynedd. The battle was fought over some magical swine Gwydion had stolen from Pryderi. Pryderi had gotten these swine from Arawn, king of Annwm, the Welsh Otherworld.

A 17th century account of the Battle of Godeu tells us that Amaethon son of Don, Gwydion's brother, had stolen a white roebuck and a whelp from Annwm. The battle was between Arawn and Amaethon. On one side was Bran, a god regularly associated with Gwynedd. In another Taliesin poem, we are told that Lleu also took part in the battle. He, too, was a figure frequently placed in northwestern Wales.

All the clues seem, therefore, to point to Gwynedd as the location of Godeu and Caer Nefenhir.

The fort in question looks to me to be Caer Nefyn Hir, the Fort of Nefyn the Tall (cf. Cai Hir, 'Caius the Tall'). This points strongly to Nefyn on the Lleyn Peninsula, not far from Peblig's Carnarvon. There are two forts at Nefyn.

The first is the hill-fort of Garn Boduan or Bodfuan, the 'Cairn of the Dwelling of Buan'. Buan was a saint in the area. The second fort at Nefyn is the promontory fort of Dinllaen, the 'Fort of the Laigin' or Leinsterman.

The goddess Modron appears in the Kat Godeu poem and it is noteworthy that the Carn Madryn fort can be found just a little southwest of Nefyn.

But if Nefyn is the location of Caer Nefyn Hir, where is Godeu?

The secret, I believe, lies in the meaning of Godeu – a meaning which will allow us to have not only one Godeu– that which was in or of Gwynedd – but two Godeus, including Urien's region of that name in the North.

The Gododdin kingdom of the North, later called Lothian, derives from a tribal name Votadini. The latter is found in early Welsh documents as Guotodin. Votadini is believed to derive from a personal name or word cognate with Irish Fothad. In Old Irish, Fothad or fothad means 'basis (?), foundation, founding, support'. But Irish fothad itself is from a root fotha, which has among its meanings 'basis', 'cause', 'charge', 'foundation', 'reason'.

I would, therefore, propose that early Welsh Godeu or godeu represents a cognate to Irish fotha and that, as such, it is effectively an abbreviation for Gododdin. Other abbreviations are found for places in the early sources. One example is the 'Aloo' used in the St. Patrick letters to Ceredig of Strathclyde. 'Aloo' here represents the first component of Alclud, the 'Rock' of Clyde.

But if Godeu = Gododdin, what is a Godeu doing on the Lleyn Peninsula in Gwynedd?

The answer to that question is simple: according to the earliest Welsh authority (Nennius in his HB), the founders of Gwynedd, led by the great Cunedda, came down from Manau Gododdin. By calling Gwynedd 'Godeu', then, the poets were ackowledging that Gododdin warriors had supposedly established a kingdom in northwest Wales.

Urien's Godeu is Gododdin in the North. The Godeu of Kat Godeu is Gwynedd.

And this brings up a related and important point: the true etymology and location of the Venerable Bede's urbs Giudi on the Firth of Forth. Giudi is found in the epic Welsh poem The Gododdin as Iodeo. The 9th century HB spells the place-name Iudeu. Finally, the Middle Irish Mothers of the Saints mentions muir n-Giudan, where muir is 'sea', a reference to the Firth of Forth.

It has become customary, for no really good reason, to identify Giudi or Iodeo with Stirling Rock.

[Stirling can be derived from the Welsh. In the Gododdin, for instance, we find stre or ystre for "border, bank; boundary, district, region; boundary dyke, rampart" (the GPC has 'battle-front' as well). Welsh stre for the first part of Stirling would leave us with –velin/-veling/-velyn/-welin to figure out. I would put forward the Welsh word gwialen, gwyalen, 'spear', found in the Gododdin poem, whose meaning (see http://www.wales.ac.uk/dictionary/pdf/GPC00 18-05.pdf) is "rod, twig, withe, sapling, cane, stick, also trans. of spear, arrow, etc."

When I proposed this etymology to Alan James of BLITON with the Scottish Place-Name Society, he responded:

"I remain very cautious about wialen, or weilein (which would be the plural of wail > gwaell but meaning much the same, some long pointed things), but I accept *[i]stre-weilein or similar is a sensible proposal.

I think, as I said last night, in a probably early name, [i]stre- is most likely to refer to a solid defensive work of some kind (rather than an abstract boundary), and, as you've mentioned, the root-sense of -wialen (and -*wailin) would have to do with sticks, stakes, etc. (especially pointed ones). So I'd interpret *[i]stre-weilein as 'a defensive work of stakes', perhaps a bank topped with a palisade, or a setting of chevaux-de-frise, most likely blocking access to the top of the rock, though I suppose there might have been some defences to control the river-crossing."

The ancient name of the Traprain Law hill-fort in the Gododdin kingdom was Dunpelder, 'Fort of the Spear-Shafts'. According to Kenneth Jackson in his 1958 paper on St. Kentigern, the volcanic formations in the Traprain summit resemble spears. Thus the spears of Stirling may also be metaphoric for the basaltic cliff.]

Andrew Breeze likens the root of Giudi to Old Welsh iud, Middle Welsh udd, 'lord', and thus interprets the name as meaning 'lord's place, place possessed by a lord'. As a purely formal etymology, this is quite acceptable.

However, as Breeze himself notes, G- has 'the sound of y in English yes.' This being so, we can take The Gododdin form Iodeo and suppose that this name entered the poem via an English source. In other words, the spelling was originally Godeo or, rather, 'Godeu'. Thus we can be fairly certain that Bede's Giudi is also Godeu. The urbs Giudi would be the 'city of the Gododdin'.

Now Bede says that urbs Giudi is 'in medio' of the Firth of Forth. This does not mean, of course, that the city is in the middle of the Firth, but rather that is it situated in the middle of the shore of the Firth in the Gododdin region. This geographical fix immediately eliminates the traditional Stirling from consideration.

However, Din Eidyn, the Dark Age capital of the Gododdin, is itself in the middle portion of the shore of the Firth. I suspect the 'city of the Gododdin' is, in fact, Din Eidyn. We need not look for urbs Giudi at Stirling or at any of the other places it has been sought (Cramond, Inveresk, etc.).

The Home of St. Patrick

A great deal of controversy still exists over the whereabouts of the home of the famous Saint Patrick. I will not here go over the various candidates, none of which have convinced the scholarly community. Instead, I will make my case for just one of these candidates, as I think new evidence can be provided in support of it.

We are told that the saint was born at 'uico [vico – "town"] bannauem taburniae (variants taberniae, thaburinde), 'where three roads meet' and that this place is 'near the western sea'. This town is otherwise known as Uentre (variants Nentriae, Nemthur).

It has long been recognized that the form 'bannauem taberniae', i.e. bannaven taberniae, shows an incorrect division of this place-name. Instead, it should read

Banna Venta Berniae

Venta is best defined thusly (from "Brittonic Language in the Old North", The Scottish Place-Name Society):

"In all the cases mentioned, a sense 'a market, a trading-place' is quite plausible, but the apparent similarity to Latin vendere, 'to sell' and its Vernacular Latin and Romance derivatives is probably misleading. Both *Bannaventa and *Glannoventa, as topographical names, might incorporate the suffix seen in the river-names above, or be based on lost river-names with that suffix. Nevertheless, Sims-Williams in APN p119 includes *Bannaventa and *Glannoventa along with the Venta group, under the sense 'market'."

Banna's etymology is as follows (also from "Brittonic Language in the Old North"):

"Non-IE *ban-, *ben- > Early Celtic *banno/ā- > Brittonic, Gaulish banno/ā-, also Gaulish benno- (in place-names) > Old Welsh bann- > (in place-name Banngolau AC s.s. 874) > middle - modern Welsh ban > middle Cornish ba[d]n > Cornish ban (see CPNE p. 16), Old Breton bann > modern Breton ban; Irish, Gaelic benn > (and Gaelic, manx beinn).

Primarily, 'a horn, prong, antler-time', so also 'a drinking-horn, a sounding-horn'. In Celtic place-names generally 'a point, promontary, spur', and in Brittonic and Pritenic place-names 'summit, top', a use which shaped the Gaelic and manx development of the dative (locative) singular beinn to an independent noun, especially in hill-names.: see G. Barrow in Uses, p. 56 (however, given the rarity of ban[n] in surviving hill-names, the influence of unrelated pen[n] may also have been a factor).

THE ARTHUR OF HISTORY

To me, it is fairly obvious that 'Uentre', first found in the Life by Muirchu, is merely a duplication in slightly corrupt form of Venta. Venta as 'market town' is a sort of Celtic substitution for Latin vicus, which has come down to us through Anglo-Saxon as wic or wick, 'market town'.

The Roman fort of Banna on the western end of Hadrian's Wall has often been pointed to as this particular Bannaventa (since the one in central England is not near the sea). The vicus or civilian settlement that surrounded the fort was quite large, so there is no problem with the vicus/venta portion of the name.

The problem is the 'Berniae', which no one has been able to make anything sensible out of. This is plainly a reference to the Tyne Gap, a narrow but distinct corridor running east-west through a lowlying gap between the uplands of the Pennines visible to north and south. The Gap spans the distance from the Tyne in the east to the Irthing in the west, and Banna/Birdoswald is right there at the western end of the Gap.

From the Electronic Dictionary of the Irish Language on the Irish word for 'gap':

bern
berna beirn berne bearn Bernai bernad bearnaidh bearna

Keywords: Gap; breach; pass; defile; position; defence; attack; refuge; breach; occupied; warri-

or; undefended; weak; position; defence; attack; position; danger; strait; fight; gap; break; flaw; drinking-horn; ungapped
Letter: B
COLUMN: 83
Line: 014
bern
ā, f. also berna iā, d and n. as. B. Chon Culaind, RC viii 54.20 (LL 13397). ds. b.¤, Sitzb. , v 93 § 30 , beirn, LL 17995 , gs. berne, FM v 1636.9 . bearn f., IGT Decl. § 39. as. Bernai, Corp. Gen. 206.17
gs. cacha bernad, LL 8030. berna f., IGT Decl. § 4. as. bearnaidh, Éigse xiv 98 § 29. gs. bearna, § 28 .

gap, breach; pass, defile; hence weak position in defence or attack: dot luid i mbernai (ar berna, v.l.) ar-mo chenn-sa thou camest into the breach against me , Sc. M² 13. is b.¤ ina coṅgaib catha a breach in their battle position , CRR 57.
do coimét na mbernd cumung robui ag techt aran slia[bh], ZCP vi 56.10 . annsa mbeirn = in the gap , Ez. xxii 30. aon- fhear faire re seasamh gach beárnan, Keat. Poems 463. ní fhūicēb-sa an b.¤ (bern-, v.l.) sin dom c[h]onāch gan caithem, ML² 1412. bearna as mo ré `a part of my life-span ', Dán Dé xvii 8 . ar bearna an bháis, DDána 30.6 . ? berna a eric, Laws ii 98.6 .i. ar in fechiumh nos gaibh, uair do rochuir ní di, 13 Comm. b.¤ na ngrás gur daingen duid refuge, IGT Decl. ex. 411.
In phrr. b.¤, berna churad, ¤míled etc. breach made or occupied by a warrior, etc.: ruc beirnd curad . . . dar cath na nAnmarcach, Cog.

188.23 . ra briss beirn míled i cath naṅGréc, LL 32300 (TTr. 1488). do bris b.¤ céit isin cath i n-urc[h]omair a aigthi `made a breach of a hundred ', Fianaig. 90.30 . berna cēt, TBC² 3672. Phr. b.¤ báegail undefended or weak position in defence or attack: afágbáil ar bernadaib báegail nó ar doirrsib aideda, Mer. Uil.² 99. ni b.¤ bægail in læch fuil and `no easy victim ', Aen. 750. See G 7.27 . Hence b.¤ position of danger, strait; fight: iarṁbrath na mb.¤, Rawl. 69 a 27 . suan ón bheirn `from fight ' (Vocab.), O'Hara 2609. re ndul san mbeirn, Dán Dé xxv 21 . gap; break, flaw in general: (expl. Bernán Brigte, name of saint's bell) foceirt forru co mmebaid ass a bernn `its gap broke out of it ' (i.e. a piece broke off), Trip. 114.14 . (of a drinking-horn) sēt blāith cen beirn `ungapped', Measgra Uí Chl. 150 § 19. an bhearn do-cháidh san chloinnse `the gap thus broken in her family ' (by a death), Aithd. D. 13.10 . dar bernadaib in inair sin, Acall. 5808 n . tar beirn na luirige, BB 435 b 46 . Compds. trias na beilgibh bernbriste dorónadh las an ordanas broken into gaps , FM vi 2300.2 . See berrbróc. beilge berncairrgidhe na banBhoirne, Hugh Roe 242.13 .

Just as importantly, the early name of Patrick in Tirechan is Magonus. The god Mogons (and variants) is found on Hadrian's Wall, especially the western half/end - where the Banna Roman fort is located. According to Celticist John Koch, the alternative name of Patrick, Magonus, might be related to this god name.

Finally, thanks to the paper by Dr. Andrew Breeze of Pamplona ("St.Patrick's Birthplace",

Wlsh Journal of Religious History, 3, 2008, pp. 58-67), I have learned of the 3rd century (?) inscription, apparently from Corbridge but now at Hexham Abbey, by a Q. Calpurnius Concessinius. Martin Charlesworth of Cambridge noticed that this Roman-period name contained both the family names of St. Patrick, whose father was Calpurnius and mother Conchessa. Q. was a prefect of an unnamed cavalry unit celebrating the slaughter of a tribal group called the Corionototae. This stone thus places both of the names of Patrick's parents near the Wall, where Banna/Birdoswald is located.

Morgan Bwlch and Bernicia

According to the Historia Brittonum, Urien of Rheged was murdered at the instigation of Morgan Bwlch, the whereabouts of whose kingdom is unknown. Several unsupportable guesses have been made.

Bwlch means 'gap, pass, breach'. It is possible, therefore, the Morgan was 'of the breach' in a heroic, military sense. However, I've demonstrated that the Tyne Gap of St. Patrick's Banna Venta (the Birdoswald fort on Hadrian's Wall) was called 'Bernia'. Kenneth Jackson long ago proposed tht Bernicia is from Celtic *Bern-acci- (cf. Irish bern, berna, 'gap, pass'). Archaeology has shown us that Bernician settlement began in the Tyne Valley. Thus in all likelihood Morgan Bwlch was a British ruler of the Tyne Gap, whose kingdom was superceded by that of the Bernician English.

THE ARTHUR OF HISTORY

Din Guayrdi/Din Guoaroy

According to the Historia Brittonum, the British name for Bamburgh was either Din ("Fort") Guayrdi or Din Guoaroy. The name has remained a problem for philologists and no satisfactory etymology has been proposed.

I would suggest the Welsh word gwyar, 'blood', plus an ethnonymic suffix. In this case, Gwyar is a proper name, possibly the mother of the famous Arthurian hero Gwalchmai. Alan James has informed me that the medial syllable would have been syncopated, so we could expect a form such as *Gwyardi. This fits Guoaroy better than, say, Welsh gwaered, 'declivity, downward slope." In the case of Guoaroy, the 'o' could be a miscopying of 'ð', 'insular d'.

Din Gwyardi, the 'Fort of the People of Gwyar.'

William of Malmesbury said that Gwalchmai had been buried at Ros (Rhos) in Wales. This may be a relocation for Ross Low at Bamburgh.

The Welsh Triads place Gwalchmai's grave on the Parret in Somerset, but this is doubtless because Gualganus, a form of his name, was wrongly linked to the Anglo-Saxon Chronicle's Cenwalh, who fought the British at that river.

CHAPTER 6

THE POWER CENTERS OF ARTHUR

Camelot

The case has often been made that Camelot is a late French form of the Romano-British Camulodunum place-name. However, archaeological evidence from both the fort on Old Lindley Moor near Slack and from the fort on Almondbury five miles from Slack (either of which may have been the ancient Camulodunum) has not revealed Dark Age occupation of these sites. The other primary candidate for Camelot is the Cadbury hill-fort by the Camel villages in Somerset. While this fort does show Dark Age occupation, its location does not match that provided for Camelot in the romances.

The first clue as to the actual whereabouts of Camelot is found in Chretien de Troyes' Knight of the Cart, which is the earliest romance to mention this site. According to Chretien, Camelot is 'in the region near Caerleon'. For some reason, most authorities have seen fit to ignore this statement, insisting that Camelot was placed near Caerleon simply because of Geoffrey of Monmouth's glorified description of the latter site as a major Arthurian centre. If we do take Chretien's statement seriously, we can for the first time arrive at a satisfactory identification of this most magical of royal cities.

The second clue to the location of Camelot is from the later romance The Quest for the Holy

THE ARTHUR OF HISTORY

Grail, wherein Arthur escorts the Grail questersfrom Camelot to a point just shy of Castle Vagan.

A third clue, from the prose Tristan, places Camelot either on or very near the sea. The last clue is from the Morte Artu; in this source, the castle of Camelot is on a river. It goes without saying that we need to look for a CASTLE or, at the very least, the site of an earlier hill-fort of some significance.

Castle Vagan is St. Fagan's Castle (W. Ffagan) four or five miles west of Cardiff. This site lies in the Ely Valley, the supposed location of the Campus Elleti of the boy Ambrosius (not the historical Ambrosius in this context, who was made into Arthur's uncle, but the 'Divine or Immortal' Lleu/Mabon; see Chapter 1 above).

According to the HB, Campus Elleti, the 'Field or Plain of Elleti', was said to be in Glywysing, the later Morgannwg/Glamorgan, which is indeed where the Ely Valley lies. Only a dozen miles separate Campus Elleti from Geoffrey of Monmouth's Caerleon.

In my opinion, Campus Elleti, with Latin Campus rendered as French Champ (the p of which is silent), became Camelot:

Cham(p) ellet(i) > Camelot

It may be that Campus Elleti, from a presumed Welsh Maes Elei or similar, was a relocation for the Moselle (Latin Mosella/Mosellae) River in

Gaul, upon which stood the Roman city of Augusta Treverorum of the Gaulish prefect A.A. and his son, St. Ambrose.

If so, this would once again confirm my identification of A.A. as a personage belonging to the 4th century.

There are two notable monuments in the lower Ely Valley. One is a Roman villa. The other is a fairly major hillfort now called Caerau. From http://caerheritageproject.com/discover/caerau-hill-fort/:

"Surrounded by housing and the A4232, Caerau hillfort is one of the largest and best preserved in South Wales. It occupies the western tip of an extensive ridge-top plateau in the western suburbs of Caerau and Ely, Cardiff, Wales. The old parish church, St Mary's, and a small ringwork, almost certainly a medieval castle site probably contemporary with the church, stand within the hillfort on the north-eastern side. Caerau Hillfort is the third largest Iron Age hillfort in Glamorgan enclosing 5.1 hectares (about the size of four football pitches). Recent excavations by Channel Four's Time Team in April 2012 showed that occupation started about 600BC and lasted, probably not continuously, into the 3rd century AD."

This is certainly the only candidate for the Camelot of the romances.

More information on the fort can be found at:

http://www.coflein.gov.uk/cy/safle/94517/man ylion/CAERAU+HILLFORT%3BCAERAU+CAMP %3BCAERAU+ELY/

Campus Elleti would refer to the flat lowland plain leading to the banks of the river to the north of the fort.

A Possible Relocation of Campus Elleti?

The problem with equating Campus Elleti with Elei involves a rather complex linguistic argument. The solution to the problem may point towards a Northern Campus Elleti – one to be found at the Corbridge Roman fort.

Dr. Graham Isaac, now with the National University of Ireland, Galway, commented as follows on the place-name Elei, , the Ely River in Glamorgan, which is associated in the 'Pa Gur' poem with Mabon servant of Uther Pendragon and is often thought to be the location of Campus Elleti:

"On Elei, it would be from the same root as Aled, Alun, Eleri, all rivers, < Celt. *al- < PIE *h2el-, 'to shine'. They are all, in different ways, 'shining rivers'. The Ravenna Cosmography's Alitacenon could be corrupt beyond redemption, but if it is accurate, then both elements are unproblematically found elsewhere: alita- 'shining [river]' gives W Aled (RN), and -cenon is a common toponym element, of admittedly uncertain meaning. [I asked Dr. Isaac about –cenon in the context of Alitacenon. If Alita- meant originally the "Shining" (-river), could not -cenon be from Proto-

Celtic *cen-je/o, "rise (from)"? In other words, Alitocenon was at the headwaters of a stream called Alito, the place where the waters of the river rose from. To which he responded, "This is not impossible."]

Elleti is probably not connected with these. The form of the name is corroborated by the instance of 'palude [Latin for "marsh" or "swamp"] Elleti' in Book of Llan Dav (148). But since both that and HB's campum Elleti are in Latin contexts, we cannot see whether the name is OW Elleti (= Elledi) or OW Ellet (= Elled) with a Latin genitive ending. Both are possible. My guess would be that OW Elleti is right. As the W suffix -i would motivate affection, so allowing the base to be posited as all-, the same as in W ar-all 'other', all-tud 'exile', Gaulish allo-, etc. Elleti would be 'other-place, place of the other side (of something)'.

There are certainly no grounds for thinking of a connection between Elleti and Elei.

For Elei, Williams is implying < *Elu-legi-. 1) I am not aware of any other instance in which the prefix El- , *Elu- is used in Welsh with a river-name. It is otherwise exclusively used with personal names. This is not damning, but it is suspicious. 2) I am not sure that the British *Elu-legi- would not in fact end up as **Ellei. I know of no precisely parallel examples offhand. But the old feminine personal name Ellylw is suggestive. This looks as though it must be < *Elu-selwi: 'Having many possessions', with the cognate of OI selb 'possession' (the exact cognate OI shelb is extant, though not as a name).

The name will have gone through the following developments *Elu-selwi:> *Elu-silwi: > *Elu-hilwi: > *El-hilw > *Ellilw (with just a long, or double,-l-) > Ellylw (now with the characteristic W -ll-). This suggests that an early Welsh double -ll- resulting from syncope becomes the later W -ll-. That is the difficulty with Williams's explanation of Elei: *Elu-legi- > *El-legi- should give > **Ellei, not Elei. At least this is how it seems to me.

The problems are different with Elleti = Elleith. The name is rare, but we have it independently in HB and in Book of Llan Dav. The spellings -e- for /ei/ and -t- for /th/ are both possible in Old Welsh, but it would be very surprising indeed if BOTH HB (and its recensions) and BLlD had spelled **Elleith as Ellet. Which makes me think that they did not, and that, in fact, they are both spelling what would be written in Modern Welsh as Elledi. And note that the HB reference to 'campum Elleti' implies a W place-name 'Maes Elledi'. I would not expect a river-name to follow 'maes'."

I would add that the Alitocenon Dr. Isaac alludes to appears to be in the Scottish Lowlands and that it is listed in the Ravenna Cosmography immediately after a Maporiton or Maporitum, the "Son's Ford". It has been suggested that this "Son's Ford" should be sought near 'locus Maponi', the "place of Maponus/Mabon [the Divine Son]", which is properly identified either with Lochmaben or the Clochmabenstane. The Ladyward Roman fort has been proposed as the most likely site. While Alitacenon's exact location is unknown, there is no reason for amending it to read Alaunacelum, as is done by A.L.F. Rivet and Colin Smith in their The Place-Names of Roman Britain.

Still, Alita- and Elleti, as just demonstrated by Dr. Isaac, have different etymologies. Thus we cannot equate Campus or Palude Elleti with Alitacenon.

We are fortunate in that the place-name Elleti may be found in the form of a personal name at the Corbridge Roman fort on Hadrian's Wall. A fragment of a large grey urn was found there bearing the name 'ALLIITIO' (Fascicule 8, RIB 2502.9; information courtesy Georgina Plowright, Curator, English Heritage Hadrian's Wall Museums). This could be the potter's name, perhaps a form of the nomen Alletius, or the name of the god portrayed on the fragment. J. Leach (in "The Smith God in Roman Britain", Archaeologia Aeliana, 40, 1962, pp. 171-184) made a case for the god in question being a divine smith, primarily due to the presence on the urn fragment of what appears to be an anvil in relief, although there were also metal workings in the neighborhood of Corbridge. Anne Ross (in her Pagan Celtic Britain, p. 253) associates the name Allitio with the same all-, "other", root Dr. Isaac linked to Elleti. She thinks Allitio may have been a warrior/smith-god and very tentatively offers "God of the Otherworld" for this theonym.

On the name 'ALLIITIO', Dr. Isaac agrees with Ross:

"Taking the double -ll- at face value, as I would be inclined to do as a working hypothesis, that would not be connected with Aled, but rather with the W all- that I have mentioned before."

Treating more fully of 'ALLIITIO' in a private communication, Georgina Plowright, Curator, English Heritage Hadrian's Wall Museums, says that the name

"...occurs twice on one piece of pottery showing feet and a base. This is always assumed to be the base of an anvil, with the feet being those of a smith god. There are a number of sherds of grey pottery from Corbridge with very distinctive applied decoration, with two recognisable themes, the smith god shown with hammer and anvil, and a wheel god who is shown with wheel and club. The fact that the wheel god is depicted by a mould suggests that this type of pottery was being made at Corbridge, though it appears on a number of other sites. The reading occurs twice on this piece of pottery, once in the frame created by the anvil base, and then on the pot below the feet of the standing figure. Another sherd showing the smith god does not have any inscription. John Dore and Stephen Johnson, who did the captions for the Corbridge gallery, have assumed that the name might be that of a potter, though RIB seems to go for either god or potter. I haven't got a copy of the Leach reference easily to hand, but my memory tells me the item should be illustrated there."

Astonishingly, of the six inscriptions for Maponus/Mabon in Roman Britain, three belong to Corbridge. These inscriptions are in the form of dedicatory altars, something not found elsewhere in Britain for Maponus.

I would propose that the Campus Elleti of Emrys in the Historia Brittonum is a relocation of an Allitio site at Corbridge. The 'Pa Gur's' Elei, associated with the 'bird of prey' Mabon, which derives from the root *al-, "to shine", represents the actual name of the Ely River, to which the Northern Campus or Palude Elleti was transferred during the usual development of myth and legend.

In passing, it may be worth noting that the (?) divine name Allitio, again according to Dr. Isaac, can be associated with Myrddin's/Merlin's Welsh nickname, Llallogan or Llallawc. This last derives from Proto-Celtic *alal(I)yo- 'another, other', cf. Old Irish arail, Middle Welsh arall (OW and MW), Middle Breton al(1)all, arall, Cornish arall. This is a reduplicated, intensive variant of Proto-Celtic *al(I)yo- 'other', cf. Old Irish aile [io], Middle Welsh eil, all-, Middle Breton eil, Cornish yl, Gaulish Allo-broges, allos, Proto-Indo-European *h2elyo- 'other', Latin alius, Go. aljis. Celtic-Iberian ailam, which has been interpreted as the Acc. of this pronoun, has also been taken to mean something like 'place, abode'.

THE ARTHUR OF HISTORY

I cannot say that Myrddin as Llallogan/Llallawc = Allitio, only that the derivation and meanings of the two names are the same.

While a construction Campus Allitio may be doubted, we can point to the Heaven-field of Bede, said to be close to Hexham, and thus quite possibly near Corbridge. Bede has this as Hefenfelth or 'caelistis campus'. The name is unlikely to be of Christain origin. Instead, we should look to the Roman period dedication (RIB 1131) at Corbridge to Caelistis Brigantia, the 'Heavenly Brigantia'. Caelistis campus would then be a field sacred to the pagan goddess of the Brigantes. In this light, a field sacred to Allitios at or near Corbridge is more plausible.

Etterby as Arthur's Burg (i.e. Stanwix)

Etterby, in the parish of Stanwix near Carlisle, was called Arthur's burg, according to Joseph Nicolson and Richard Burn's History and Antiuities of the County of Westmorland and Cumberland, Vol. 2:

"Etterby in old writings is called Arthuriburgum, which seems to imply that it had been a considerable village. Some affirm, that it took its name from Arthur king of the Britons, who was in this country about the year 550 pursuing his victories over the Danes and Norwegians. But there are no remains of antiquity at or near this place to justify such a conjecture."

Nicolson and Burn may have been correct in their assessment of Etterby as wholly lacking 'remains of antiquity'. The evidence from excavation has been too slender to confirm a tentative suggestion as to what kind of Roman camp – if any - may once have existed at Etterby. While it has been suggested that there might be a Roman camp at Etterby, no evidence for this has been found.

However, there is some evidence for the neighboring Stanwix Roman fort continuing into the post-Roman period. Thus, if there is a connection with 'Arthur', it should be attached to Stanwix, rather than to Etterby.

The timber features at Stanwix are fairly recent discoveries. Most of the excavations there have been unpublished, so when archaeologists talk about the timber buildings these may be more examples of timber hall-like structures (such as those from the Birdoswald Roman fort). There is always a hope that the Stanwix excavations revealing the late Roman/sub-Roman timber structures will be published, but in the meantime it is interesting to know that the Carlisle Millenium Project excavation report will be available in the near future (the Carlisle Roman fort being just a stone's throw across the river from Stanwix), and very late timber structures were also found there.

The truly amazing thing about the 9.79 acre fort of Stanwix, whose Romano-British name was Uxellodunum, the 'High Fort', is that it is exactly between the forts of Camboglanna, where Arthur died, and Aballava on the western end of the Wall (see Chapter 7 below for my discussion of

Aballava as 'Avalon').

This large fort also housed a force of one-thousand cavalry, the Ala Petriana, the only milliary ala ('wing') in the whole of Britain. The Petriana's presence at Stanwix accounts for the name of this fort in the late 4th/early 5th century 'Notitia Dignatatum' – Petrianis. Titus Pomponius Petra, a distinguished former commander of the unit, gave his name to the ala.

Roman historian Sheppard Frere nicely sums up the strategic importance of this fort:

"The western sector of the Wall was the most dangerous... both on account of the nature of the ground and because of the hostile population beyond it. It is not surprising to find, then, that at Stanwix near Carlisle was stationed the Ala Petriana... Such regiments are always found on the post of danger; and the prefect of this Ala was the senior officer in the whole of the wall garrison. Here, then, lay Command headquarters, and it has been shown that a signaling system existed along the road from Carlisle to York, which would enable the prefect at Stanwix to communicate with the legionary legate at York in a matter of minutes."

The fort lay on a fine natural platform today occupied by Stanwix Church and Stanwix House, a little over 8 miles from Castlesteads (Camboglanna).

To the south lies the steep bank falling to the River Eden, while the land falls somewhat more gently to the north. Little is known about the fort apart from its defences. The south-west angle tower, south wall and east wall were traced in 1940, with the north wall being located in 1984. This was uncovered in the grounds of the Cumbria Park Hotel. A length of wall was subsequently left exposed for public viewing and the line of the wall marked out by setts; the exposed portion of wall lies close to the north-west corner of the fort. This and the south-west corner, a low rise in the churchyard, are the only remains visible today. Brampton Road lies more or less on the line of the south defences, with Well Lane marking the east defences.

The northern end of Romanby Close lies approximately at the north-east corner of the fort. The northern defences consisted of a stone wall with a clay rampart backing, fronted by two ditches; an interval tower was also found. The north wall was 5 ft 8 in wide with a chambered base course above the footings on the north side; the rampart backing was at least 11 ft 6 in wide.

To the south of the tower lay a feature tentatively identified as an oven. The fort appears to be an addition to the Wall which was located in 1932-4 a little to the south of the north fort wall, with the north lip of its ditch found in 1984 to lie under the interval tower. A few meters further south, a turf deposit, probably a rampart, was recorded in 1997. No other trace has been discovered at Stanwix of a turf-and-timber fort, but the known fort is clearly later than the replacement of the Turf Wall in stone.

The causeway over the south ditch was located beside Brampton Road in 1933. This was placed centrally in the southern defences, but this in itself gives little indication of the internal arrangements, which might have been unusual in such a large fort. Little is known of the interior buildings. A series of four parallel walls, possibly representing two barracks-blocks and lying towards the north fort wall, were examined in the school yard in 1934. A large granary was located further south in 1940.

The Archaeological Evidence for Stanwix as Arthur's Power Center

In this section I will be discussing the case that has been recently made by Ken Dark of the University of Reading for the sub-Roman (i.e. 5th-6th century CE) re-use of Hadrian's Wall, as well as of forts along the Wall and in the adjacent tribal territory of the ancient Brigantian kingdom.

According to Dark, from whose paper I will liberally quote:

"... eight fourth-century fort sites on, or close to, the line of Hadrian's Wall have produced, albeit sometimes slight, evidence of fifth -sixth-century use. Nor is this simply a reflection of a pattern found father north; for no Roman fort site in what is now Scotland has any plausible evidence of immediately post-Roman use. Thus the situation to the north of the Wall is similar to that found in Wales.

What is more surprising still is the character of the reuse found on the line of the Wall. Two sites, Housesteads and Corbridge, have evidence not only of internal occupation, but of refortification; at Birdoswald there are the well known 'halls', while at Chesterholma Class-I inscribed stone of the late fifth or early sixth century come from the immediate vicinity of the fort. At South Shields there is also evidence of re-fortification, and there is an external inhumation cemetery. Another Class-I stone was identified by C.A.R. Radford at Castlesteads [I have rendered the inscription of this stone above in Chapter 3].

At Binchester immediately to the south of the Wall, and at Carvoran, Benwell and Housesteads on its line, there are early Anglo- Saxon burials or finds, while at Chestersand Chesterholm (perhaps sixth century) Anglo - Saxon annular brooches come from within the forts, although these may be somewhat later in date than the other material so far mentioned.

At the western terminal of the Wall, a town-site, Carlisle, though not necessarily primarily military in the Late Roman period, has also produced substantial evidence of sub-Roman occupation, with continued use of Roman-period buildings into the fifth, if not sixth, century.

Many scholars accept that Carlisle was part of the late fourth-century Wall-system, perhaps even its headquarters, and at Corbridge, the other town-site intimately connected with the Wall, fifth -and sixth century material has also been found, including, perhaps, evidence of continuing British and Anglo-Saxon use. In the North as a whole, fifth- or sixth-century evidence from what had been Late Roman towns is not common. York, Aldborough, Malton, and Catterick are our only other examples. Two of these sites (York and Malton) were part of the same Late Roman military command as Hadrian's Wall: that of the Dux Britanniarum.

It is interesting that, of the sites at Manchester and Ribchester– between the Mersey and Carlislethe only fort-sites known to have possible fifth or sixth -century evidence – Ribchester was not only part of the command of the Dux Britanniarum, but also listed as per lineum ualli in the Notitia Dignitatum. It is, therefore, remarkable that out of the twelve fourth-century Roman military sites in northern and western Britain to have produced convincingly datable structural, artefactual, or stratigraphic evidence of fifth-or sixth-century occupation, eleven were, almost certainly, part of the Late Roman military command.

Eight of these were probably within the same part of that command, and eight comprise a linear group (the only regional group) which stretches along the whole line of Hadrian's Wall from east to west. The two more substantial late fourth- century settlements adjacent to the Wall – Carlisle and Corbridge– have also produced fifth- and sixth-century evidence and two of the other towns with such evidence were also late fourth-century strategic centres under the military command of the Dux."

After setting forth these facts, and discussing them, Dr. Dark offers a rather revolutionary idea:

"Although it is difficult, therefore, to ascertain whether the military project which I have described was the work of an alliance or a north British kingdom or over-kingdom, there does seem to be reason to suppose that it may have represented a post-Roman form of the command of the Dux Britanniarum...

This archaeological pattern, however it is interpreted, is of the greatest interest not only to the study of the fifth-and sixth- century north of Britain, but to that of the end of Roman Britain and the end of the Western Roman Empire as a whole. It may provide evidence for the latest functioning military command of Roman derivation in the West, outside the areas of Eastern Imperial control, and could be testimony to the largest Insular Celtic kingdom known to us."

In another paper, Ken and S.P. Dark rebut P.J. Casey's argument for a re -interpretation of the reuse and re-fortification of the Wall and its associated forts. His conclusion for this paper reads as follows:

"If one adopts the interpretation that the Wall forts were reused in the later fifth-early sixth century for a series of sub-Roman secular elite settlements, thenthe associated problems involved in explaining this new evidence of occupation at that time disappear...

THE ARTHUR OF HISTORY

So, the interpretation that the Wall became a series of secular elite settlements, discontinuous from the Late Roman activity at the forts within which they were sited, is compatible with the evidence of pollen analysis, while the alternative interpretations are both rendered unlikely by it.
This does not, of course, make the suggestion that this reoccupation represents the sub-Roman reconstruction of the Command of the Dux Britanniarum any more likely, but the pattern on which that interpretation is based has been strengthened, rather than weakened, by the new archaeological data, whilst the evidence also hints at a similar reoccupation with regard to the signal stations of the Yorkshire coast and their headquarters at Malton.

Perhaps, then, at last one is able to see answers to many of the most pressing questions regarding what happened in north Britain, and more specifically on Hadrian's Wall, in the fifth and sixth centuries...

The answer to all of these questions may lie in the rise and fall of a reconstructed Late Roman military command, unique in Britain, which was organized in a sub-Roman fashion reliant upon the loyal warbands of warrior aristocrats (and Anglo-Saxon mercenaries) rather than paid regular soldiers. The organizing authority of this system, probably a king of the sub-Roman Brigantes, assigned a politico-military role to the defended homesteads of these elites, and (as in the location of churches at disused forts, through land-grants?) positioned these at what had been Roman fort sites, but which were (at least substantially) deserted by the time when they were reused in this way. Thus, the 'Late Roman' Wall communities dispersed during the first half of the fifth century, but the Wall – andperhaps the north generally – was redefended inthe later fifth and early-mid sixth century onvery different lines, yet not completely without regard for the Late Roman past."

I would add only that it is my belief this 'king' of the sub-Roman Brigantes whom Dr. Dark proposes was none other than the dux bellorum Arthur.

An Arthur placed at Stanwix makes a great deal of sense when we place these two forts in the context of the Arthurian battles as I have outlined those in Chapter 3 above. These battle site identifications (taken from the list in the HB, supplemented by the Welsh Annals) shows a range of conflict extending from Buxton in the south to a the Forth in the north, with the majority of the contests against the enemy being fought along or just off the Roman Dere Street from York northwards. The site of Arthur's death is in a fort only a few miles to the east of Stanwix and we will see in the next chapter that the location of his grave is most likely at a Roman fort just a few miles west of Stanwix.

The battle site identifications were made solely on linguistic grounds, but end up revealing a quite plausible geographical and thus strategic scenario for Arthur's military activities.

THE ARTHUR OF HISTORY

I will consider another candidate for Arthur's capital in Appendix II below – one that perhaps holds even more promise than Stanwix.

CHAPTER 7

THE GRAVE OF ARTHUR

It is not my purpose in this chapter to deal with what I consider to be the misidentification of Glastonbury with Avalon. Others have presented a detailed case against the fraudulent claim of Glastonbury as the final resting place of King Arthur, and I added some of my own arguments in my previous book, The Mysteries of Avalon.

Here I wish to restrict my attention to the only known place in Britain to actually have born the name Avalon prior to the time of Arthur as well as to this place's proximity to both Arthur's Camlann at Castlesteads and his possible ruling center towards the west end of Hadrian's Wall.

Obviously, the possible location of his grave at Avalon is of great interest to anyone seeking to demonstrate the reality of a historical Arthur. Geoffrey of Monmouth's 'Insula Avallonis' or 'Isle of Avalon' is held by most Arthurian scholars to be a purely mythological designation - no matter where one chooses to localize it.

From a philological standpoint, the –on terminal of Avallon or Avalon demands an original terminal fronted by a broad vowel. Thus there is a problem trying to equate the word with Welsh afallen, 'apple tree', or Cornish avallen. This problem can be overcome in two ways: 1) by evoking an attested Continental place-name, e.g. Aballone, modern Avallon, in France or by 2) allowing for the possibility that the plural form of

Welsh afal, afalau, cf. Cornish avalow and Breton avalou, at some point underwent a fairly common miscopying of u/w as n.

As it happens, the only known site in all of Roman Britain to bear an 'Avalon' name is the Aballava fort at Burgh-By-Sands, 5. miles west of Stanwix on Hadrian's Wall. This fort is under 14 miles west of Castlesteads. The name Aballava is found listed in the various early sources in the following forms:

Aballava – Rudge Cup and Amiens patera
Aballavensium – RIB inscription No. 883
Avalana, Avalava – Ravenna Cosmography
Aballaba – Notitia Dignitatum

It is the one spelling in the Ravenna Cosmography that stands out here. The v of Aballava/Avalava has been rendered as an n, yielding the spelling Avalana. This is exactly the type of spelling we would need to end up with Geoffrey of Monmouth's Latinized Avallonis.

The Celtic derivational suffix –ava of Aballava, British *-aua, is now found in the –au of Welsh, giving as a meaning for Insula Avallonis 'Island of the Apple-trees'.

An Arthur who fell at Camlann/Camboglanna at Castlesteads could easily have been carted along the Roman road or brought down the river system in this region to Burgh-By-Sands.

Camboglanna is on the Irthing, a tributary of the Eden River. The Eden empties into the Solway

Firth very near Aballava/Avalana.

Two dedications to a goddess Latis were made at the Birdoswald Roman fort, 7 miles east of Castlesteads, and at Aballava. The first (RIB 1897) is addressed to DIA LATI and the second to DEAE LATI. Latis comes from a British root similar to Proto-Celtic *lati-, 'liquid, fluid', and Proto-Indo-European *lat-, 'wet'. Some authorities have seen in her a goddess of beer (cf. Old Irish laith, 'ale, liquor'), but here she is manifestly a goddess of open bodies of fresh water, i.e. she is a literal 'Lady of the Lake'. Burgh-By-Sands was, in fact, surrounded by vast marshlands. Although these lands have long since been drained, the area is still called 'Burgh Marsh'. We can be fairly certain, then, that the Avalon fort was on an island of sorts, the true 'Insula' of Geoffrey of Monmouth's apple-tree Otherworld.

Topography dictated the position of the Aballava fort. There was an important crossing of the Solway at Burgh and the existence of this crossing may have influenced the siting of the Roman fort here. The fort sits atop a low hill on the highest ground at the east end of the village. The church sits within the south-east corner of the fort and is partly built of Roman stones. The modern road lies on the line of the Wall. Burgh is one of the least explored and understood of all the forts on the Wall. Although earlier visitors presumed a fort here, no remains were visible.

Excavations north of the church in 1922, when a new burial ground was formed, resulted in the location of the east wall, 6-7 ft thick, with an earth backing, and the east gate of the fort, with a road leading out. Within the fort, stone buildings running north-south were interpreted as barracks-blocks. The Roman levels and buildings were all badly preserved.

The sketch plan of the site prepared on the basis of these discoveries suggests a fort measuring 520 ft north-south by 410 ft east-west, giving an area of nearly 5 acres. Excavations on several occasions between 1978 and 2002 south and east of the fort has led to the discovery of buildings, presumably of the civil settlement. The bath-house, south of the fort, was destroyed in making the canal, itself replaced by the railway line, now also abandoned. Further south, the tombstone of a Dacian tribesman may indicate the location of the cemetery. Recent excavations have failed to clarify the location, size and date of the Wall fort at Burgh. We do know the stone fort lay astride the Wall, but the Wall ditch was infilled and re-cut before it was constructed. It is possible that the fort to the south of the Wall at Moorhouse was retained for some time before being succeeded by a replacement astride the Wall.

As stated above, the actual Roman period cemetary at Burgh-By-Sands/Aballava is said have been to the south of the fort. When I enquired about the tombstone of the Dacian tribesman found in this cemetery, Tim Padley at the Tullie House Museum in Carlisle informed me of the discovery of two other fragments. All three are listed in the Roman Inscriptions of Britain as follows:

2046 (tombstone)
...
IVL PII... TINVS CIVES DACVS
2047 (tombstone) D M S
...
2048 (tombstone) VII

Alas, according to Mr. Padley, the placement of the cemetary to the 'south of the fort' puts it, in his words, 'near the vallum, possibly destroyed by the canal and railway.'

The tombstone fragments were in the care of Tullie House when they disappeared.

While it is impossible to know whether Arthur was buried in the Roman period cemetary of the Aballava fort, this cemetary must remain a primary candidate for the location of his grave.

THE ARTHUR OF HISTORY

AFTERWORD

THE KING WHO WILL BE AGAIN

In this book, I have revealed a chieftain named Arthur/Ceido who fought a dozen or so Dark Age battles against the Saxons before being taken to Avalon/Burgh-By-Sands to be with the Goddess of the Lake in death.

But for many – and this is as true for those who lived shortly after Arthur's time as it is for us of the modern era – Arthur does not lie in a grave at Avalon. Instead, he continues to live in a curious limbo, a place composed of equal parts continued literary and artistic invention, entertainment and gaming industry exploitation, academic specialization and Celtic/Neo-Pagan Reconstructionism.

Under the latter guise, the shift away from an Arthur who is an attestable personage has, ironically, paralleled the renewed academic insistence on the non-historicity of this northern chieftain. For while academics now, almost without exception, view Arthur as a purely legendary figure derived from folklore and developed through the medium of medieval romance, the Celtic Reconstructionists reinterpret this greatest of British heroes in a multitude of ways.

Some still hold to the age-old Messianic view that Arthur is merely being healed of his wounds by Morgan le Fay in a spiritual versus a physical Avalon. They believe that he will, in the time of

Britain's most dire need (or, indeed, in the time of Mankind's most dire need), come forth to defeat some monstrous evil. Others seek to trace their bloodlines to Arthur, to his knights, to Avalon priestesses or to Grail kings in order to inherit the immense spiritual heritage that resides in the Arthurian story.

There are even individuals who claim to be Arthur or, perhaps, a reincarnation of him. I have personally met a man who makes a very decent living 'channeling' the spirit of Merlin, a spirit who with profound and pithy pronouncements advises clients on how to go about conducting their daily lives and business affairs.

This 'New Aging' of Arthur would seem to be a harmless phenomenon, serving the positive function of bringing many new members into the Arthurian fold and contributing to a heightened level of spiritual awareness, as well as fostering a sense of 'connectedness' with ancestors and nature in an uniquely Celtic fashion. But today's pagans need to be careful not to create alarming amounts of contrived information masquerading as inspired truth or subjective revelation that might feed naive, inwardly-focused belief systems. These last distract us from objectively obtained realities.

As a person who himself is not immune to mystical experience, let me hasten to add that I am not advocating spiritual matters be excluded from the Arthurian orbit. Cutting off this aspect of our humanity is not only undesirable, but thoroughly impractical. The human psyche simply does not work this way. What I am pleading for is a separation of what is acknowledged as fact or reasonable conjecture from what is intuited as having religious significance. Or, to be more precise, what we choose to adhere to as tenets of belief should be based upon or extrapolated from what we know on a rational level, rather than the reverse. Be spiritual about things/concepts that actually exist or once existed. Do not give in to the temptation to readily accept as the basis for belief anything that contradicts or ignores a body of evidence assembled by decades or centuries of intense scientific effort.

St. Augustine said "I believe so that I may know". This is a dangerous credo. Instead, "We should know so that we can believe."

Furthemore, any belief system, no matter how self-satisfying, should be eschewed by anyone who truly cares about Arthur and things Arthurian if it intentionally seeks to hide potential truths from us or block us from paths that may lead to genuine understanding of deeper matters.

Belief systems of this sort are usually promulgated by cult leaders who created them, i.e. those with their own often sinister agendas and need for control and profit. Any cultic use of the Arthurian tradition would be, in essence, antithetical to that tradition. Still, there always remains the danger that unusually susceptible minds could be programmed to make use of the Arthurian tradition in an unacceptable fashion.

Those who wish to be latter-day Knights of the Round Table must guard against such a misuse of a code of conduct that, as it has been refined since the Middle Ages, promises compassionate treatment of all persons, places and things.

Most marvelous of all would be the development of a joint spiritual, aesthetic and scientific mindset whose sole unifying purpose was to increase and enhance opportunities available for those daring individuals questing after a real Arthur. If there were a core group of people of this ilk or predisposition, the whole thrust of exploration into the possibility of an historical Arthur would not only be forever altered, but in my opinion strengthened a hundred-fold. A solitary vision forged from divergent approaches and applied with discipline and conviction to the problem of Arthur is what is required for us to be able to bring Arthur back from the Otherworld of disbelief in which current scholarly opinion has consigned him. Like the sword Excalibur, made in Avalon and rising up through the water and mist of the lake, a new paradigm in the field of Arthurian Studies must be inaugurated, implemented and sustained.

Of course, our chances of finding Arthur – of ultimately proving his historicity – depend almost entirely on finding an intact, inscribed tombstone somewhere in the vicinity of the Burgh-By-Sands fort. Natural processes such as erosion, combined with man's radical alteration of the environment and his accompanying willful destruction and occasional subsequent reuse of ancient monuments, makes the likelihood of our finding a memorial stone set up for Arthur of the 6th century an extremely doubtful proposition. Still, foolish as it may sound, it is just such an artifact that we need to be searching for. The discovery of the Cynric/Cunorix Stone at Wroxeter gives us hope that a similar stone for Arthur may someday be found at Burgh-By-Sands.

New labour saving methods of investigation now at our disposal, e.g. ground penetrating radar, allow for less costly, less invasive, less timeconsuming, less bureaucratic means of finally locating and determining the nature and extent of the Burgh-By-Sand's Roman cemetery. Whole memorial stones or fragments of such stones may have been incorporated into walls or buildings.

A careful visual inspection of these kinds of structures may yield significant findings. Members of the community of Burgh-By-Sands could be canvassed regarding any stones in their possession that bear what appears to be ancient writing. A correspondent who lives in the town quipped that someone could be using an inscribed stone for a door-stop! Then again, Arthur's Stone may be awaiting discovery in the foundation of the church or in the stall of a neighboring farmer's barn.

It is also vital to attempt to ascertain exactly where the missing Burgh-By-Sand tombstone fragments were found. This would entail determining who now possesses the fragments – if the parties concerned or their immediate descendents are still alive. Interviews with such people might shed important light on the cemetary's location.

If private collectors of Roman artifacts can be made aware of the importance of these stones, perhaps they would be forthcoming with valuable information, especially if they were allowed to do so anonymously or were granted immunity from prosecution in the event the artifacts in question had been obtained illegally.

Archaeological excavation work is always the final resort. All too often it is undertaken in advance of a major building project as an imposed afterthought. Time, money and personnel constraints add up to produce what is all too often a hurried, haphazard and incomplete dig.
Only rarely is a full-scale archaeological project proposed and executed because a site is chosen in advance for its own intrinsic merits.

I would put forward the Burgh-By-Sands Roman period cemetery as an archaeological site of astounding potential. Just imagine what it would be like to discover Arthur's memorial stone! Granted, we cannot know if a tombstone was ever made for Arthur. Nor can we know whether such a stone, if made, has survived the intervening centuries. And even if such a stone were found, nay-sayers would insist that just because a Arthur of the right period could now be placed at Burgh-By-Sands, it does not follow that such an individual was THE Arthur.
However, if there is any truth to the Avalon story, and Arthur was brought to Burgh-By-Sands

to be buried in sacred ground, then there is a remote chance that some trace of his presence at this fort has been preserved. And it seems to me that there must be someone out there whose destiny it is to find that trace.

Someone who wishes to prove, once and for all, that Arthur did exist.

APPENDIX I

Cadburys and Badburys

"Right at the South end of South Cadbury Church stands Camelot. This was once a noted town or castle, set on a real peak of a hill, and with marvellously strong natural defences..... The only information local people can offer is that they have heard that Arthur frequently came to Camelot." John Leland's ITINERARY

"The fact that Baddanburg refers at least in three cases to prehistoric camps is remarkable and may suggest that Badda was a legendary hero, who was associated with ancient camps." Eilert Ekwall, THE CONCISE OXFORD DICTIONARY OF ENGLISH PLACE-NAMES

Of the Devon and Somerset Cadbury hill-forts, we are generally told these are from a 'Cada's fort'. Cada is a presumed English personal name. However, the British prince Cadwy, Latinized Cato or Catovii or Catovi, son of the Dumnonian king Geraint, is known to have shared rule with Arthur of a fort called Dindraethou somewhere in Devon or Somerset. This same fort is mentioned in the Irish Cormac's Glossary as Dun/Dinn Tradui/Tredui or the ' Triple-fossed fort ' of Crimthann the Great, son of Fidach, king of Ireland. Dindraethou, called Cair Draitou in the Nennius list of British cities, is transparently 'Fort of the Strands/Beaches. This place has somewhat haphazardly been identified with Dunster where, however, no fort or corresponding place-name exists. The only significant fort with a triple ditch in this region is Cadbury or Cada's burg, specifically Cadbury Castle in Somerset. This fort has thus been identified as Dinn Tradui.

The other candidate for Dun Tradui or Dindraethou is the Maes Knoll fort at the end of Dundry Hill ridge in Avon. Dundry is a place-name of uncertain derivation. Mills says simply OE dun + draeg (following Ekwall), but adds "Alternatively perhaps a Celtic name for Dundry Hill from *din 'fort' with another element."

The meaning "fort of the strands or beaches" does not work for Dunster, Cadbury Castle or Dundry. How do we resolve this difficulty?

Nennius wrote his History in the latter part of the first half of the 9th century. Cormac's Glossary is put in the early 10th. Also, we must give preference to a British source naming British places over an Irish source doing the same. Thus there is little reason to trust the Dun Tradui as the correct form of this place-name. Undoubtedly, Dun Tradui or the Triple-Fossed Fort is an Irish attempt to render Cair/Dindraitou/draethou.

Where, then, is this Fort of the Beaches/Strands? Firstly, we must remember that the sea level has changed substantially from the Dark Ages to the present time. For example, much of the Somerset Levels were underwater. So it is distinctly possible that a fort which was once on the beach is now far from the water.

Cadbury Castle was not on the water – although in Roman times the sea encroached almost as far as Ilchester (see Map 1:16 in Rivet and Smith's AN ATLAS OF ROMAN BRITAIN). Cadbury Camp at Tickenham in North Somerset was just a bit too far north to have been considered 'coastal'. However, the Cadbury Hill fort just north of Congresbury would have been right on this earlier coastline. As this fits a fort on the beaches or strands, and has the necessary Cadwy name, I without hesitation identify this fort as Dindraethou.

From Pastscape on Cadbury Hill Camp:

"A univallate Iron Age earthwork with steep natural slopes on all sides except the east. An entrance, with probableguard-chambers, on the south-east. The ramparts, mostly tumbled down the steep slopes, had been timber-framed. A quarry pit, abundant pottery, post holes and about 830 slingstones were found.

Two hearths and an associated rectangular building dated between about 430 AD and 450 AD were uncovered under the ramparts of the fourth phase.

Between about 450 AD and 480 AD stone-based defences faced with turf and timber were erected within the perimeter of the Iron Age ramparts and, probably later, a bastion added.

The final phase, between about 480 AD and the early 6th century, overlay the collapsed defences of the previous phase. The remains of eight huts, two circular, 15m in diameter, and a "longhouse" 8m by 3m were found. Finds included imported Mediterranean ware, local and Gaulish pottery, Roman and later beads, glass, bricks, bronze and iron objects, and 3, possibly 4, type G penannular brooches."

The Cungar of Congresbury was remembered as a saint, although his origin is obscure. Some have sought to identify him with Cyngar son of Geraint, but the feast days are not the same (Bartrum). Given Arthur's presence at Cadbury/Congresbury, I would suggest the name was associated with the Congair (Irish genealogy) or Cincar/Cyngar (Welsh version) that was the son of the Dyfed Voteporix. This particular Cyngar was born c. 510, and his grandson was Arthur of Dyfed. This would suggest the placement of the much later Arthur (b. 560) with Cadwy son of Geraint at this hill-fort.

If the Cadbury forts in Devon and Somerset were named for Cadwy son of Geraint, and this name was altered to English Cada, might we apply the same principle to the various Badbury forts, which are supposedly named for an otherwise completely unknown English hero Badda?

There are five Badburys (according to Ekwall), four of which have ancient fortifications next to them. It has been suggested (see, for example, Richard Coates, "Middle English Badde and Related Puzzles", NOWELLE, Vol II, February 1988) that Badda could be a hypocoristic form (or diminutive, 'pet' form) of Beada, a name which is derived from the following:

BEADO, beadu; g. d. beadowe, beadwe, beaduwe; f. Battle, war, slaughter, cruelty; pugna, strages :-- Gúþ-Geáta leód, beadwe heard the War-Goths' prince, brave in battle, Beo. Th. 3082; B. 1539. Wit ðære beadwo begen ne onþungan we both prospered not in the war, Exon. 129b; Th. 497, 2; Rä. 85, 23. Beorn beaduwe heard a man brave in battle, Andr. Kmbl. 1963; An. 984. Ðú þeóde bealdest to beadowe thou encouragest the people to slaughter, Andr. Kmbl. 2373; An. 1188. [O. H. Ger. badu-, pato-: O. Nrs. böð, f. a battle: Sansk. badh to kill.] - Bosworth and Toller dictionary

If so, we would have the remarkable coincidence of the Badbury hill-forts being derived from a name meaning battle, just as is the case with the Cadbury forts. However, although with the Cadbury forts we can safely associate them with a known early ruler of Dumnonia, the Badbury forts cover such a vast area that to do the same with them hardly seems tenable. I think a derivation depending on Badda being from Beada is very doubtful. For one, there is the problem of the –dd- versus the –d-, something treated of by Coates and others. Coates opts (see bellow) for an early word with the same basic meaning as our modern English 'bad', although the presence of this word in Old English is not attested, and no etymology for it is known.

A friend has recently asked me about the possible significance of Gildas's stragis, 'slaughter', used by this author in the context of the Badon battle. This is, of course, the famous battle of

THE ARTHUR OF HISTORY

Badon Hill, usually ascribed to Arthur of legendary fame. We see above that beado does include in its meanings 'slaughter'/Latin strages. This does not get us past the problem noticed early on by linguists (and reiterated recently via personal communication by Dr. Graham Isaac of The National University of Ireland, Galway) that Badon must come from English bathum/batham/bathan, 'baths', and cannot come from Baddan-. Baddan would have yielded 'Baton' in the British. [Pure contextual comparison yields the same verdict, as Badon is spelled 'Badonis' in the Arthurian section of Nennius, and exactly the same way in the 'Marvels of Britain' section, where it is indisputably given as the name for Bath in Somerset. I've shown that Arthur's Bath is more likely the batham/'baths' city of Buxton in the Peak.]

One important fact has been overlooked in all this: if we compare the line of Badbury forts from south-central England to east-central England (see p. 62 of Leslie Alcock's 'Arthur's Britain') with A) the line that runs through the Roman period tribal kingdoms of the Durotriges, Dobunni and Corieltauvi to the west and Belgae, Atrebates, Catuvellauni and Iceni to the east (see. p. 154 of Jones and Mattingly's "An Atlas of Roman Britain") and with B) the line the runs along the border of late fifth century England, showing the Anglo-Saxon cemeteries to the east and the British-held territory to the west (see p. 52 of N.J. Higham's 'King Arthur: Myth-Making and History"), a startling correspondence emerges. All these boundaries or frontier zones match up almost perfectly.

Is this a coincidence and thus merely illusory? Perhaps. But it would be to our advantage to investigate this correspondence more closely, just in case it helps us untangle the mystery of the etymology of Badda/Baddan-.

First, to the problem discussed by Coates, viz. the ultimate origin of the word 'bad', which would seem to be related to Badda/Baddan-. If we connect an unattested Old English precursor of ME badde with the Indo-European root bhoi-/bhai-/bhi-, 'to fear', we can establish a further link to Latin foedus, "foul, filthy, loathsome, repulsive, ugly, unseemly, detestable, abominable, horrible' (Lewis and Short Dictionary, via Perseus). I do not think this is an unreasonable supposition.

The full Pokorny listing for this root is as follows (http://dnghu.org/indoeuropean.html):>

"Root / lemma: bhōi- : bhəi- : bhī- (bhiiə-)

English meaning: to fear

German meaning: `sich fürchten'

Material: Old Indian bháyatē `be afraid' (from *bhəi̯etai = slav. bojetъ), av. bayente, byente `they are in fear', mpers. bēsānd `they are in fear' (uriran. *bai-sk̂-); Old Indian bibhéti `be afraid', sek. to initial Perf. m. Prösensbed. bibháya `I am in fear' (bibhīyāt, bibhītana, abibhēt, participle bibhīvān = av. biwivā̊ were afraid'); Old Indian bhiyāná-ḥ `were afraid'; bhī́-

ḥf., bhīti-ḥf. (: lett. Inf. bîtiês) `fear', bhīmá-ḥ`dreadful', bhītá-ḥ`were afraid, horrified', bhīrú-ḥ`timorous, shy, coward' (if r = idg. 1, changing through ablaut with lit. báilė, bailùs); npers. bāk `fear' (from *bháyaka-); with idg. simplification of āi to ā before consonant here Old Indian bhāmaḥ perhaps `fierceness, fury', bhāmitá-ḥ `fierce, grim'.

Gr. πίθηκος, πίθων m. `ape' (from *πιθος `ugly', zero grade *bhidh-).

Lat. foedus (*bhoidhos) `foul, filthy, horrible, disgusting'.

Ahd. bibēn, as. bibōn, ags. beofian, aisl. bifa, -aða and bifra (these in ending directed after *titrōn `tremble') to urg. *ƀiƀai-mi; *ƀiƀōn is probably only after to the other coexistence from -ōn- and -ēn- secondary verb besides one from the Perfect form developed grade *ƀiƀēn .

Bsl. originally present *bhəi̯ō-, preterit-stem *bhii̯ā-, Inf. *bhītēi; Old Prussian biātwei `fear, dread', kausat. pobaiint `punish, curse'; lit. bijaũs, bijótis (also not reflexive) `be afraid', lett. bîstuôs, bijuôs, bîtiês and bijājuôs, bijâtiês `be afraid'; lit. baijùs `dreadful, terrible, hideous'; baidaũ, -ýti `frighten', lett. baīdu, baīdȳt and biêdêt `daunt, scare';

Maybe alb. geg. mbajt `be afraid', nuk ma mban `I am afraid'

in addition lit. baisà `fright' (*baid-s-ā), baisùs `terrible, horrid', baisióti `smudge, besmear' (and

Old Church Slavic běsъ `devil', *běd-sъ); lit. báimė `fear'; báilė ds. (bailus `timorous').

Old ChurchSlavic bojǫ, bojati sę `be afraid'.

Further formation *bhii̯-es-, *bhīs- in Old Indian bhyásatē `be afraid', udbhyása-ḥ`be afraidd', av. Perf. biwivāŋha (i.e. biwyāŋha) `stimulated fright, was dreadful'; Old Indian bhīṣayatē `frightens', bhīṣaṇa-ḥ `causing fright';

ahd. bīsa `north-east wind', bisōn `run around madly', bēr `boar' etc lead to a germ.*bīs-, *bīz- `storm ahead jumpily'; compare Wißmann Nom. postverb. 78.

References: WP. II 124 f., 186, WH. I 522 f., Trautmann 24, Kluge11 under Biese.

Page(s): 161-162"

But this brings in another important point. The idea that all these forts – a couple of them being quite beautiful, and very impressive – were all somehow "bad" does not make much sense. We could say that they were "bad" in the sense that they belonged to the enemy, but again, this is hardly convincing. For this reason I would mention another word from Latin that is spelled EXACTLY the same as the foedus just mentioned: foedus, "a league, treaty, compact, alliance."

This second foedus comes from the following Indo-European root:

"Root / lemma: bheidh-1

English meaning: to advise, force

German meaning: `jemandem zureden, zwingen', med. `sich einreden lassen, vertrauen'

Material: Gr. πείθομαι `lets me persuade, follow' (Aor.ἐπιθόμην, hom. πεπιθεῖν, πιθέσθαι; Perf. πέποιθα `trust'), Akt. (sek.) πείθω, Aor.ἔπεισα `persuade, convince', πειθώ, -οῦς `persuasion', πιστός (for *φιστος) `reliable, loyal, faithful, relying', πίστις, -ιος, -εως `loyalty, reliance', hom.ἐν πείσῃ `in reassurance' (*πειθ-σ-);

alb. bē f. `oath, vow, pledge' (*bhoidhā = Old Church Slavic běda `need'), ostgeg. per-bej `curse, hex' (in addition neologism bese f. `faith, belief, pact, covenant, loyalty');

Note: alb. bē f. `oath' derived from a truncated alb. betim `oath'

maybe TN illyr. Besoi : alb. besoj `believe, have faith'

lat. fīdō, -ere, fīsus sum `to trust, believe, confide in' (fīsus is to- participle), fīdus `reliable'; foedus (*bhoidhos), by Ennius fīdus (*bheidhos) n. `trusty, true, faithful, sure', fidēs `trust, confidence, reliance, belief, faith', Dius Fidius `the god of faith, a surname of Jupiter'; umbr. combifiatu (*bhidhiā-) `you shall trust, confide, rely upon, believe, be assured'; about osk. Fiisiais, umbr. Fise, Fiso, Fisovio- s. WH. I 494;

Note:

Alb. alb. fē, fēja 'religion', fejonj 'perform engagement ceremony (marriage vowsö)' : AN fed, OFr. feid, feit : lat. fides;

got. baidjan 'constrain, oblige', aisl. beiđa, ags. bædan, ahd. beitten 'urge, press, push, arrogate' = abg. causative běždǫ, běditi 'constrain, oblige', poběditi 'defeat, conquer', běda f. 'need';

here probably also got. beidan 'wait, hold on', aisl. bīđa, ags. bīdan, ahd. bītan ds., schweiz. beite = ahd. beitten, but in the meaning 'wait, hold on'. basic meaning 'await' from 'trust' or 'oneself constrain, oblige'.

References: WP. II 139 f., 185 f., WH. I 493 f.

Page(s): 117"

From this root comes Old English baedde, a thing required, tribute, baedde, solicited, baedan, to constrain, compel, require, solicit, bad, a pledge, stake, a thing distrained, badian, to pledge.

What I would like to propose for the Badda/Baddan- fort names is that they do NOT actually come from an AS form of ME badde, our 'bad', but instead from the attested Old English root that may be compared with that which yielded Latin foedus, fides, etc.

Richard Coates long ago ("On some Controversy surrounding Gewissae/Gewissei, Cerdic and

THE ARTHUR OF HISTORY

Ceawlin", Nomina 13, 1989-90) showed that the Gewessei of Dark Age Britain "... look very much like the 'known ones', in the sense of those who are known of or known about, i.e. the people of whom you have certain knowledge." I showed subsequently that the Gewessei were, in fact, Irish mercenaries or "federates" utilized by Vortigern against his various enemies, including other Britons. As such, these Gewessei were opposed to the other Celts, who were 'wealhas' or Welsh, a Saxon term meaning stranger, foreigner and hence enemy.

In the Roman period, the term used for such "barbarian" federates was "foederati", from L. foedus. So what exactly am I suggesting here? Simply this: that Badda as a personal name is a reflection of a foederatus or 'federated' mercenary who was stationed along a line of forts which for some time marked the frontier zone between the Anglo-Saxons and the Britons. I am NOT saying we are dealing here with the SAME single federated mercenary raised to hero status, but rather a general personification of the foederati.

Badda, then, is representative of the foederati, probably Saxon federates who guarded the border region in sub-Roman England.

As a comparison to Badda, a name derived (?) from the AS bad, 'pledge', I would point to the Scandinavian Varangian mercenaries of the Byzantine empire. The root of the name Varangian is Norse var, 'pledge', as in the pledge a foreign Rus/Swedish Viking gives when taking service with a new lord by a treaty of fealty to him (see H.S. Falk & A. Torp, Norwegisch-dänisches etymologisches Wörterbuch, 1911, pp. 1403–4; J. de Vries, Altnordisches etymologisches Wörterbuch, 1962, pp. 671–2; S. Blöndal & B. Benedikz, The Varangians of Byzantium, 1978, p. 4). Badda would be something like 'the pledged one' or the 'one who pledged himself'.

Some might ask why, if the line of Badbury forts was what the Romans referred to as a limes, there were foederati stationed here. Shouldn't we expect instead limitanei?

Actually, no. To quote from Nora Chadwick's "Celtic Britain (New York, 1963):

"During this closing phase of the Occupation some new officials appear in the records of affairs in Britain, probably connected with the defensive measures taken on her behalf by the usurper Constantine on the eve of his departure. Here our chief guide is the Notitia Dignitatum. This document enables us to watch a process of devolution at work in Britain analogous in many respects to that which had already taken place on the Continent since the reform measures of the Roman Army by Diocletian (286-305) and Constantine (305-307). Briefly stated, this process entails the withdrawal and supplanting of the Roman sedentary troops massed on the frontier, known as limitanei (L. limes, a 'frontier'), by a local militia, consisting of foederati or federate native troops..."

POSTSCRIPT:

Since writing this Appendix, I have been sent an article from Somerset Archaeology and Natural History Vol 134 1990, pp. 81-93, "The frontier Zone and the Siege of Mount Badon: A Review of the Evidene for Their Location", by Tim and Annette Burkitt. This article very nicely details in texts and maps the frontier zone that existed at the time of the Battle of Badon. My thanks to Gail Griffith of SANHS for providing me with the piece.

APPENDIX II

Birdoswald Rather Than Stanwix as Arthur's Capital?

If, as I have discussed in the main text above, the Irthing River and Valley may preserve an English form of a regional designation Arthwys, and Arthwys personified as an ancestor is to be associated with Arthur, then the possibility that the Irthing region was the actual power center of Arthur must be considered.

I've elsewhere made the case for Stanwix, site of the 1,000 strong cavalry regiment garrisoned at the Uxellodunum Roman fort, being Arthur's probable capital. However, there is a site in the Irthing Valley that shows sub-Roman activity whose dating is preferable to that of Stanwix: the Banna Roman fort at Birdoswald.

The possible late timber structures at Stanwix do not appear to have continued in use into the first quarter of the 6th century, something which is necessary for a historical Arthur who perished c. 537 at the Camboglanna/Camlann (Castlesteads) Roman fort – itself on a tributary of the Irthing. But some remarkable timber structures at Birdoswald do meet this critical requirement.

From Excavations at the Hadrian's Wall fort of Birdoswald (Banna), Cumbria: 1996–2000 by Tony Wilmott, Hilary Cool and Jeremy Evans with contributions by: K F Hartley, Katie Hirst,

Jacquline I McKinley, Quita Mould, David Shotter, A G Vince, D F Williams and S H Willis, in HADRIAN'S WALL: ARCHAEOLOGICAL RESEARCH BY ENGLISH HERITAGE 1976–2000:

"Periods 5 and 6: sub- and post-Roman

The later 4th century and later periods at Birdoswald have been extensively discussed elsewhere (Wilmott 1997a, 203–231). In summary, Period 5 represented the late-Roman transition between the Roman occupation of Period 4, and Period 6, which may be described as 'non-Roman' in character. During this Period, the ventilated sub-floor of the south granary was backfilled and the flagstone floor re-laid. The latest coin from this fill was dated to 348, giving a terminus post quem for this work. Silty layers were succeeded by a re-laid patchy stone floor, incorporating two hearths at one end of the building, around which were found highstatus items such as a gold earring, a glass finger ring and a worn, silver Theodosian coin (388–95).

At the same time, the north granary roof collapsed (terminus post quem 350–3) and the building was robbed of its walling stone and floor flags, the former sub- floor being used as a dumping area. The coinage from these dumps ran on from 348–378, and the finds also included a small penannular brooch of a characteristic sub-Roman type (Snape 1992, 158).

'Non-Roman' Period 6 was characterised by the erection of timber structures over the remains of the north granary and over the roads of the fort. The first major building was post-built with most of the posts placed in shallow postholes located in the tops of the robbed granary walls. A new floor of re-used flagstones over facing stones was laid over the roof tile spread from the building's collapse. This building was larger than the granary.

A small service building was constructed as a post-built lean-to against the inner side of the fort wall south of the west gate. The second phase of timber buildings saw the erection of a freestanding, framed building founded on post-pads.

The south wall was on the site of the former granary, but the north wall on the former via principalis, aligned with the spina of the west gate, thus covering the road inside the blocked south gate portal. This building was surface-built, as were two small structures founded on surface-laid sleeper beams on the intervallum road. Apparently at the same time, the west gate was provided with a new, timber-built outer portal, possibly allowing gates to be hung to open outwards, and thus to be more defensible.

Dating for Period 6 is problematic. The south granary was clearly re-used, possibly as a hall building, with the hearths at the western end provided for the leading figures in the fort community.

If the timber structures were the functional successors of this building, as seems likely, the terminus post quem for the first is c 388–95. As the Theodosian coin was worn, however, this could be assumed to be later, perhaps c 420. An estimated life of 50 years for each building would bring the close of occupation to c 520.

The excavations reported above had little to contribute to knowledge of these phases because the barrack areas within the fort were heavily truncated and activity in the extra-mural areas ended in the later 3rd century. The sole evidence thought to relate to Period 5 to survive in the north-west praetentura was the final phase of Building 803, the officer's house in the north-west corner of the fort. This building clearly survived in use longer than the adjacent structure to the east. The terminus post quem for the apsidal structure within this building is 330–70, which places it within the same period as the late 4th-century re-use of the south horreum (Wilmott 1997a, 203–6). It is tentatively inte preted as a possible church. Similar interpretations have been advanced for an apsidal structure built at Housesteads on a street in the north-west corner (Crow 1995, 95–6), and at Vindolanda, within the courtyard of the praetorium (Birley et al 1998, 20–1).

At South Shields there is some evidence that the principia forecourt was transformed into a church in the late 4th century (Bidwell and Speak 1994a, 102–3). Also at Vindolanda the early Christian tombstone of Brigomaglos, dated c 500, indicates a late Roman/early post-Roman Christian presence (Jackson 1982, 62), as does other recently discovered artefactual evidence.

Long-cist graves (all empty) have been claimed adjacent to the church at Housesteads, at Sewingshields (Crow and Jackson 1997, 66–7) and east of Birdoswald (Wilmott 2000, fig 16). It is possible that Birdoswald was one of a number of forts that persisted as a Christian centre."

Mr. Wilmott was kind enough to answer my questions regarding some possible sub-Roman graves found at Birdoswald. From his personal correspondence:

"The long cist found to the east of the fort seems to be a one-off, though admittedly there has been no further work in this area to confirm a cemetery or otherwise.

However I can give you further info. In 2011 we did a small excavation of the known Roman cemetery to the west of the vicus (there was a threat of loss to river cliff erosion). There we found an enclosure containing largely 2nd-3rd century cremations. In the entrance to the enclosure, effectively blocking the entrance, were two inhumation graves. There was no bone in either due to the acid conditions. One appears to have been double. This contained a flat pillow-stone in the half which would have held the taller individual. The second grave was pebble lined in the manner of a long cist. One of these cut the fill of the enclosure ditch, from which came Crambeck parchment ware dated AD 375 +. So a 5th century date is the best fit.

Analysis towards publication continues on this project.

I tried, as you will have seen, to summarise some of the thinking in my excavation report in 1987, but this was largely in context with a recent (at the time) book, and also the fact that the moment the hall buildings were found the press invoked Arthur based on the old identification of Birdoswald/ Camboglanna, disproved, of course by Hassall in 1976. I wanted to get the story of the archaeological findings out without this overlay, as the archaeological community were at first sceptical of the evidence in the ground.

When the exercise basilica was reported I had a phone call from an Irish nun who identified the word 'basilica' with church and asked if I'd found the basilica of St Patrick. It seems that you are going to give a rather more reasoned analysis of the material."

We therefore have at Birdoswald structures which indicate the presence of someone LIKE Arthur at Arthur's time. The Irthing River, whose region was perhaps designated as Arthwys, the place of the Bear, may have received its name from Arthur himself, the 'Bear-king'. The fact that Camlann or Castlesteads was only several miles to the west in the same river valley system adds weight to an argument seeking to place Arthur at Birdoswald.

APPENDIX III

Camlan and the Grave of Osfran's Son

The purpose of this essay is to prove, once and for all, where Arthur's Camlann battle site was located. Or, more accurately, where Welsh tradition happen to place it!

It is fairly well known that the Welsh record seven survivors of Camlann. Yet, to my knowledge, no one has sought to plot these personages out on a map. To do so may help us pinpoint a geographical region in which Camlann was believed to be situated.

One of the seven – Geneid Hir – it a difficult and otherwise unknown name. P.C. Bartram (in "A Welsh Classical Dictionary: People in History and Legend up to about A.D. 1000) suggests the name may be corrupt and offers an unlikely identification with a personage named Eueyd or Euehyd Hir (often rendered Hefeydd). However, I would see in Geneid 'Cannaid', "white, bright, shining, pure, clean, radiant," an epithet substituted for the original title Ceimiad, 'Pilgrim', of St. Elian. Elian had churches on Mon/Anglesey and in Rhos, Gwynedd.

Sandde Bryd Angel looks to be a pun for the Afon Angell, Aberangell, etc., places immediately to the south of the Camlan on the Afon Dyfi in Merionethshire.

THE ARTHUR OF HISTORY

Morfran son of Tegid is from Llyn Tegid, now Bala Lake in Gwynedd.

St. Cynfelyn is of Llancynfelyn in Ceredigion just below the Afon Dyfi.

St. Cedwyn of Llangedwyn in Powys, while somewhat further removed than the rest, is still in NW Wales.

St. Pedrog of Llanbedrog is on the Lleyn Peninsula in Gwynedd, just opposite the three Camlans in Merionethshire.

St. Derfel Gadarn is at Llandderfel near Bala Lake in Gwynedd.

Needless to say, if we "triangulate" with all these names/places, we find at the center the three Merionethshire Camlans.

So which one is the right one?

Only one way to know for sure: we must find the Camlann that is claimed as the gravesite of Osfran's son. This reference comes from the 'Stanzas of the Graves:'

Bet mab Ossvran yg Camlan,
Gvydi llauer kywlavan...

The grave of Osfran's son is at Camlan,
After many a slaughter...

["The Black Books of Carmarthen 'Stanzas of the Graves', Thomas Jones, Sir John Rhys Memorial

Lecture, 1967, Critical Text and Translation.]

While –fran of Osfran looks like Bran or 'Raven', the Os- does not look at all right for a Welsh name. I suspected Ys- and after a first search failed, I defaulted to bryn or 'hill' as the original of –bran. Thus I was looking for an Ysbryn.

And I actually found him – or, rather, it! [See "An Inventory of the Ancient Monuments in Wales and Monmouthshire: VI – County of Merioneth", p. 98, RCAHMW, 1921.]

On the Mawddach River in Merionethshire there is a Foel Ispri. It used to be Moel Ysbryn and was the legendary residence of Ysbryn Gawr or Ysbryn the Giant. If we go north on the Mawddach we run into its tributary the Afon Gamlan, i.e. the Water of the Crooked Bank.

In a section of my book THE MYSTERIES OF AVALON, I included the following note detailing one of the supposed sites for Arthur's grave. As it happens, this tradition matches the one that places Camlan on the Afon Gamlan.

A Note on Northwestern Wales as the Site of Arthur's Grave

There are a few Camlans/Gamlans in north-western Wales or Gwynedd. The presence of these sites has prompted various Arthurian scholars to propose that Arthur fought his last and fatal battle in this region. The modern champions of this notion are Steve Blake and Scott Lloyd, whose book PENDRAGON: THE

THE ARTHUR OF HISTORY

DEFINITIVE ACCOUNT OF THE ORIGINS OF KING ARTHUR, was released in 2003 by Lyons press.

We cannot ignore these Camlans or Gamlans (the most noteworthy being the Afon Gamlan, a river) when searching for a historical Arthur. Unlike the placement of Camlan (or Camlann) in Cornwall, something done by Geoffrey of Monmouth in his HISTORY OF THE KINGS OF BRITAIN, Gwynedd can claim to possess real candidates for Arthur's final battle site. The only other known site that qualifies linguistically is much further north – Camboglanna on Hadrian's Wall, which I have discussed above in Chaper 3.

Blake and Lloyd place their trust in a very late medieval source, the VERA HISTORIA MORTE DE ARTHURI, a work dated in extant MSS. to c. 1300, although perhaps to originals dating between 1199 and 1203. According to Blake and Lloyd, the VERA HISTORIA probably was written in Gwynedd. I will not contest this point, as it may well be correct.

The importance of the VERA HISTORIA lies in its placement of Arthur's interment – and thus of Avalon – in Gwynedd. Although Blake and Lloyd are familiar with the Gwynedd tradition which places Arthur's grave at Carnedd Arthur near Cwm-y-llan or Cym Llan (an error for Cwm Llem, the Valley of the river Llem), they choose to ignore this bit of folklore and instead settle on Tre Beddau near Llanfair, well to the east on the Conwy River, as the actual burial place of the king. They deduce this from the fact that the VERA HISTORIA states that the grave is near a church of St. Mary (in Welsh, Llan-fair), and that archaeologists have recently uncovered a Dark Age or 6th century cemetery at Tre Beddau.

[Note: Cwm Llan is a very clumsy attempt at rendering Camlan, and is obviously spurious tradition.]

Unfortunately, the authors of PENDRAGON also choose to ignore the description of the burial place of Arthur as preserved in the VERA HISTORIA. In their own words, the burial of Arthur after Camlan is told as follows:

"... the VERA HISTORIA describes the funeral of Arthur as taking place at a chapel dedicated to the Virgin, the entrance to which was so narrow that the mourners had to enter by first forcing their shoulder into the gap and then dragging the rest of their body through the opening. While the funeral took place inside the chapel, a large storm blew up and a mist descended, so thick that is was impossible to see the body of Arthur – which had been left outside, as it would not fit into the chapel. Following the storm the mourners came out to find that the body had gone and the tomb prepared for Arthur was sealed shut, 'such that it rather seemed to be one single stone'."

Now, this passage quite obviously DOES NOT portray a 6th century Christian cemetery. Rather, it is a fitting description of a 'chapel' comparable to the "Green Chapel' of SIR

GAWAIN AND THE GREEN KNIGHT. In other words, the said 'chapel' is a Neolithic chambered tomb, whose passage is so tight as to barely allow the entrance of the mourners.

Furthermore, we are talking about TWO conjoined passage tombs – one that is the chapel of the Virgin, and the other which mysteriously receives the body of King Arthur. In all of Gwynedd, there is only one such ancient monument: that of the double chamber tomb of Dyffryn Ardudwy not far west of the Afon Gamlan.

One of the two chambers of Dyffryn Ardudwy is actually known as Coetan Arthur or Arthur's Quoit. The "Virgin" is here a Christian embellishment on what would have been a pagan goddess associated with the Otherworld site.

The grave of Arthur discussed in the VERA HISTORIA is thus a product of folklore only. It can thus be dismissed as an actual grave of Arthur.

Granted, we cannot so easily dismiss the Camlans/Gamlans in northwestern Wales. Since writing this, Dr. Jessica Hughes of CADW has sent me information via snail-mail that adds important details to the description of the Dyffryn Ardudwy chambered tombs. To quote Dr. Hughes:

"The Chambered tomb at Dyffryn Ardudwy has been known as Coetan Arthur in the past, indeed antiquarian reports of the site refer to

Dyffryn as 'Coetan Arthur'. However, the name appears to refer to the whole of the monument as opposed to a particular chamber. Interestingly (and maybe somewhat confusingly), one mile to the east of Dyffryn lies another chambered tomb known as 'Cors-y-Gedal'. This was also known in the past as 'Coetan Arthur'... Regarding whether there is a church of St. Mary in proximity to Dyffryn Ardudwy, I have found a church 4 miles north of Dyffryn in the village of Llanfair. "

The enclosed Detail Report on this Church of St. Mary states that Llanfair was dedicated to Mary "by at least the 12c when Gerald of Wales and Archbishop Bladwin stayed there in 1188..."

Here is the COFLEIN listing for the second chambered cairn:

http://www.coflein.gov.uk/en/site/93724/details/CORS-Y-GEDOL%2C+BURIAL+CHAMBER/

"A rather tapering rectilinear cairn, c.31m NESW by 14.5m, showing at its eastern end a number of orthostats, partly supporting a tipped capstone, c.3.6m by 3.0m & 0.45m thick: a spindlewhorl, thought to be IA, is said to have come from under the capstone."

Both of these chambered tombs are directly west of the Afon Gamlan.

Conclusion Regarding Arthur's Welsh Camlan

THE ARTHUR OF HISTORY

The next question, of course, is what Arthur was it who died at the Afon Gamlan – assuming the Welsh tradition is historical in nature? It can't be a Northern Arthur. It could be Arthur of Dyfed, but if so, the 537 A.D. date given for Camlann in the Welsh Annals is a gross error.

There is an Arthur son of Bicoir 'the Briton' in the Irish sources, but this may well be Arthur of Dyfed, whose father's name occurs in a number of variants, including Petuir, which could have become Bicoir. Complicating all of this is the presence of a Dark Age Beccurus stone a couple dozen kilometers NW of the Afon Gamlan at Gesail Gyfarch, Penmorfa. It is tempting to see in this Beccurus the Bicoir (genitive form of the name?) father of Arthur.

The problem is that both Arthur of Dyfed and Arthur son of Bicoir, whether the same man or different, have floruits well after the Badon and Camlann dates claimed for Arthur in the Welsh Annals. The most logical explanation for this is not that the Welsh Afon Gamlan is the wrong location for the Camlann battle, and that the Welsh have relocated the site here from Camboglanna on Hadrian's Wall.

Numerous such relocations have been found in the early Welsh sources. To cite merely one example, Rhydderch of Strathclyde is said in the "Stanzas of the Graves" to lie at Abererch on the Lleyn Peninsula in Gwynedd.

BIBLIOGRAPHY

Alcock, Leslie. Arthur's Britain: History and Archaeology A.D. 367-634. 1990, Penguin, Hammondsworth.

Austen, Paul S. Recent Excavations on Hadrian's Wall at Burgh-By-Sands in Transactions of the Cumberland & Westmorland Antiquarian & Archaeological Society Vol. XCIV. 1994, Alan Sutton Publishing Ltd, Stroud.

Bannerman, John. Studies in the History of Dalriada. 1974, Scottish Academic Press, Edinburgh and London.

Barber, John, & Elaine Lawes-Martay and Jeremy Milln. The Linear Earthworks of Southern Scotland: Survey and Classification in Transactions of the Dumfriesshire and Galloway Natural History and Antiquarian Society, Series III, LXXIII, 1999.

Bartrum, Peter C. A Welsh Classical Dictionary: People in History and Legend up to about A.D. 1000. 1993, The National Library of Wales.

_____. Welsh Genealogies A.D. 300-1400 (8 vols). 1974, 1980, Cardiff.

Bidwell, Paul (ed). Hadrian's Wall 1989-1999: A Summary of Recent Excavations and Research prepared for The Twelfth Pilgrimage of Hadrian's Wall, 14-21 August 1999. 1999, Carlisle: Cumberland and Westmorland Antiquarian and Archaeological Society and the Society of Antiquaries of Newcastle upon Tyne.

Bieler, Ludwig (ed. & tr.). The Patrician Texts in the Book of Armagh. Scriptores Latini Hiberniae 10. 1979, Dublin Institute for Advanced Studies, Dublin.

Breeze, Andrew C. Pennango Near Hawick and Welsh Angau 'Death'. 2002, Northern History 39.

_____. Some Celtic Place-Names of Scotland: Ptolemy's Verubium Promontorium, Bede's Urbs Giudi, Mendick, Minto, and Panlathy. 2004, Scottish Language 23.

Breeze, David J. J. Collingwood Bruce's Handbook to the Roman Wall. 2006, 14th Edn. Society of Antiquries of Newcastle upon Tyne.

Bromwich, Rachel. Trioedd Ynys Prydein: The Welsh Triads. 1978, 2nd Edn, The University of Wales Press, Cardiff.

_____, & A.O.H. Jarman, & Brynley F. Roberts (eds.). The Arthur of the Welsh. 1999, The University of Wales Press, Cardiff.

_____, & R. Brinley Jones (eds.). Asudiaethau ar yr Hengerdd. 1978, University of Wales Press, Cardiff.

Brown, T. Craig. The History of Selkirkshire or Chronicles of Ettrick Forest, Vol. 1. 1886, David Douglas, Edinburgh.

Cable, James (tr.). The Death of King Arthur. 1975, Penguin Books.

Calise, J.M.P., Pictish Sourcebook: Documents of Medieval Legend and Dark Age History. 2020, Greenwood Publishing Group.

Cameron, Kenneth. The Place-Names of Derbyshire, Vol. 1. 1959, Cambridge University Press, Cambirdge.

Cessford, Craig. Post-Severan Cramond, The Heroic Age, Issue 4 (Winter) 2001. [See Supplementary Online Bibliography]

Clarke, Basil. Calidon and the Caledonian Forest, in The Bulletin of the Board of Celtic Studies, Vol. XXIII, Part III, November 1969.

Coates, Richard. Middle English Badde and Related Puzzles in North-Western European Language Evolution, Vol. 11, February 1988.

_____, On some Controversy surrounding Gewissae/Gewissei, Cerdic and Ceawlin in Nomina 13, 1989-90.

Collingwood, R.G. Explorations at the Roman fort of Burgh-By-Sands in Transactions of the Cumberland & Westmorland Antiquarian & Archaeological Society, Vol. XXII, 1923.

Collingwood, W. G. Arthur's Battles in Antiquity 3, 1929, 292-298.

Cooper, Nicholas J. The Archaeology of the East Midlands: An Archaeological Resource Assessment and Research Agenda, in Leicester Archaeology Monograph No. 13. 2006, University of Leicester, Leicester.

Crawford, O. G. S. Arthur and his Battles in Antiquity 9, 1935, 277.

Curtis, Renee L. The Romance of Tristan. 1994, Oxford University Press, Oxford.

Dark, K.R. A Sub-Roman Re-Defense of Hadrian's Wall? In Britannia Vol. XXIII, 1993, 111-120.

_____, & S.P. New Archaeological and Palynological Evidence for a Sub-Roman Reoccupation of Hadrian's Wall, in Archaeologia Aeliana, 5th Series, XXIV, 1196, 57-72.

Diehl, Ernst. Inscriptiones Latinae Christianae Veteres Vol. I-III. 1926-1931, Berlin.

Dyer, James. The Penguin Guide to Prehistoric England and Wales. 1982, Penguin Books, New York and London.

Ekwall, Eilert. English River-Names. 1928, Clarendon Press, Oxford.

_____. The Concise Oxford Dictionary of English Place-Names, 4th Edn. 1977, Clarendon Press, Oxford.

Field, P.J.C. King Arthur's Battles, An Inaugural Lecture, School of English & Linguistics, University of Wales, Bangor, 1995.

Foster, Idris, and Glyn Daniel. Prehistoric and Early Wales. 1965, Routledge and Kegan Paul, London.

Fraser, James E., From Caledonia to Pictland: Scotland to 795. 2009, Oxford University Press.

Frere, Sheppard. Britannia: A History of Roman Britain. 1987, Routledge and Kegan Paul, London and New York.

Gover, J.E.B., A. Mawer & F.M. Stenton (eds). The Place-Names of Wiltshire in Journal of the English Place-Name Society 16. Cambridge: 1939.

Hall, J. R. Clark, & H.D. Merritt. A Concise Anglo-Saxon Dictionary (4th edn). 1969, Cambridge University Press, Cambridge.

Handford, S.A. (ed), & Mattingly, H.(tr). The Agricola and the Germania. 1971, Penguin Classics.

Haycock, Marged (ed). Blodeugerdd Barddas o Ganu Crefyddol Cynnar. 1994, Barddas, Swansea.

Higham, N.J. King Arthur: Myth-Making and History. 2002, London and New York.

_____, & Barri Jones. The Carvetii. 1991, Alan Sutton Publishing Ltd., Wolfboro Falls.

Hunt, August. The Mysteries of Avalon: A Primer on Arthurian Druidism. 2011

Jackson, Kenneth Hurlstone. Arthur's Battle of Breguoin in Antiquity 23, 1949, 48-9.

_____, Once Again Arthur's Battles in Modern Philology 43, 1945-6, 45-57.

_____, The Site of Mount Badon in Journal of Celtic Studies II, 1953-8, 152-5.

Jarman, A.O.H. Aneirin: Y Gododdin, Britain's Oldest Herioc Poem. 2005, Gomer Press, Llandysul.

_____, Llyfr Du Caerfyrddin. 1982, University of Wales Press, Cardiff.

Jarrett, Michael G. Non-legionary Troops In Roman Britain: Part One, The Units in Britannia, Vol. XXV, 1995, 35-77.

Kennedy, W.N. Remarks on the Ancient Barrier Called 'The Catrail', with Plans in Proceedings of the Society of Antiquaries of Scotland, 1857-1860, 117-121.

Kibler, William W. & Carleton W. Carroll (tr). Chretien De Troyes: Arthurian Romances. 1991, Penguin Books.

Langham, Mike & Colin Wells. Buxton: A Pictorial History. 1993, Phillimore, Chichester.

Leach, John. The Smith God in Roman Britain in Archaeologia Aeliana Series 4 Volume 40, 1962, 171-184.

Loomis, Roger Sherman. Arthurian Literature in the Middle Ages: A Collaborative History. 1959, Oxford University Press, Oxford.

Mattaraso, P.M. The Quest of the Holy Grail. 1969, Penguin Books.

Mawr, Allen. The Place-Names of Northumberland and Durham. 1920, Cambridge University Press, Cambridge.

McCarthy, Mike. Roman Carlisle & the Lands of the Solway. 2002, Tempus Publishing Ltd., Stroud.

Mills, A.D. A Dictionary of English Place-Names. 1991, Oxford University Press, Oxford.
Morris, John. Nennius: British History and The Welsh Annals. 1980, Phillimore, London and Chichester.
_____. The Age of Arthur: A History of the British Isles from 350-650. 1995, Phoenix, London.
Nicolson, Joseph & Richard Burn. History & Antiquities of the County of Westmorland and Cumberland, Vol. 2. 1977.
Ottaway, Patrick. Roman York. 2004, Tempus.
Padel, O.J., & D.N. Parsons (eds). A Commodity of Good Names: Essays in Honour of Margaret Gelling. 2008, Shaun Tyas, Stamford.
Radford, C.A.R. The Early Inscriptions of Dumnonia. 1975, Cornwall Archaeological Society, Redruth.
Rivet, A.L.F., & Colin Smith. The Place-Names of Roman Britain. 1982, B.T. Batsford Ltd., London.
Ross, Anne. Pagan Celtic Britain: Studies in Iconography and Tradition. 1996, Academy Chicago Publishers, Chicago.
Rowland, Jenny. Early Welsh Saga Poetry: a Study and Edition of the Englynion. 1990, D. S. Brewer, Cambridge.
Shotter, David. Romans and Britons in North-West England. 1993, Centre for North-West Regional Studies, University of Lancaster.
Thomas, Charles. And Shall These Mute Stones Speak? Post-Roman Inscriptions in Western Britain. 1994, University of Wales Press, Cardiff.
Tolstoy, Nikolai. Nennius, Chapter Fifty-Six in Bulletin of the Board of Celtic Studies Vol. 19, 1960-2.

Walker, J., & L. Walker & R. Sheppard, assisted by J. Brown, and K. Swainson. Buxton, The Natural Baths: An Assessment for High Peak Borough Council, 2nd edn. Nottingham: Trent & Peak Archaeological Trust, May 1994.
Watson, Godfrey & Goodwife Hot & Others. Northumberland's Past as Shown in its Place Names. 1970, Oriel Press, Newcastle-Upon-Tyne.
Watson, William J. The History of the Celtic Place-Names of Scotland. 1926, Edinburgh and London.
Williams, Ifor. Canu Aneirin: Poetical Work of Aneirin. 1938, Cardiff.
_____, Enawau Lleoedd 40. 1945, Liverpool.
_____ (ed). The Poems of Taliesin. 1968, The Dublin Institute for Advanced Studies, Dublin.
Winterbottom, Michael. Gildas: The Ruin of Britain and Other Works. 1978, Phillimore, London and Chichester.
Wright, R.P., & K.H. Jackson. A Late Inscription From Wroxeter in The Antiquaries Journal, Vol. XLVIII, 1968
Zimmer, Stefan. The Name of Arthur – a New Etymology in Journal of Celtic Linguistics, 13, 2009, pp. 131-6.

ONLINE RESOURCES

http://darkavalonbooks.posterous.com

http://www.vortigernstudies.org.uk/vortigernhomepage.htm

http://www.britannia.com/history/index.html

http://www.mun.ca/mst/heroicage/

http://www.pastscape.org.uk/

http://www.rcahms.gov.uk/

http://www.rcahmw.gov.uk/hi/rng/Home/

http://www.roman-britain.org

http://www.ucc.ie/celt/

http://www.ucl.ac.uk/archaeology/cisp/database/

Printed in Great Britain
by Amazon